Fifty States of Bacon

I.M. Bacon

haggart
enterprises, llc

© Copyright 2015 Haggart Enterprises, LLC

Cover art by Greg P. Haggart

Edited by Nancy Haggart

Printed in the United States of America

Published by Haggart Enterprises, LLC and Create Space
A publication of The United States of Bacon

ISBN-13: 978-1511406239
ISBN-10: 1511406232

CONTENTS

About The United States of Bacon............................5

Introduction...5

Alabama...7

Alaska..9

Arizona..12

Arkansas...14

California...17

Colorado...20

Connecticut..23

Delaware...26

Florida..28

Georgia...30

Hawaii..33

Idaho...36

Illinois...38

Indiana...42

Iowa..45

Kansas..48

Kentucky...51

Louisiana...54

Maine...57

Maryland...60

Massachusetts..64

Michigan..67

Minnesota..70

Mississippi..73

Missouri..75

Montana..78

Nebraska..81

Nevada..85

New Hampshire...87

New Jersey...90

New Mexico..92

New York...95

North Carolina..97

North Dakota..99

Ohio...102

Oklahoma..104

Oregon..108

Pennsylvania..111

Rhode Island..115

South Carolina..118

South Dakota..121

Tennessee..123

Texas..126

Utah...129

Vermont..131

Virginia...135

Washington..137

West Virginia..141

Wisconsin..144

Wyoming...146

Other Books...149

Notes..150

About the United States of Bacon

The United States of Bacon introduces, Fifty States of Bacon; a recipe and factoid book on bacon for every conversation and to make delicious treats.

If you love bacon as much as we do, please join us in our community on Facebook at www.facebook.com/USBacon.

Visit our clothing shop at www.theunitedstatesofbacon.com and order bacon clothing to reveal your love for bacon.

Introduction

The mighty meat candy boar its way through history when the Romans boiled bacon with figs and pepper sauce: since then by the 1600s bacon was easily brined as a dietary staple for European peasants, by the 1770s John Harris opened the first commercial bacon-making company in the United Kingdom. Oscar Mayer introduced pre-packaged, pre-sliced bacon in 1924 to the American public beginning America's obsession with pig candy with nearly three million pork-producing companies, churning out billions of pounds of bacon a year. Now America's obsession with bacon has opened new avenues of flavor with bacon bits, Bakon Vodka, bacon salt, baconnaise, bacon lip balm, and bacon lube. But the obsession for bacon never stopped there. Now we see chocolate-covered bacon, bacon lollipops, bacon flavored breath mints, and bacon ice cream. Bacon has also inspired inventers with the first alarm clock in 2009 which cooks bacon to wake you instead of using an annoying alarm. Americans cannot get enough of bacon and their eagerness to use the tasty meat in any food to enhance dishes proves bacon's worth.

In addition, have you had sleepless nights because all you can think about is that meat candy humanity calls, bacon? The very sound of the word sends true believers a chill up their spine and gets their saliva juices rolling. There is no question that bacon is thee meat of all meats that make meats taste better. In the wise words of Jim Gaffigan, "Put bacon on a potato and you have an entrée." Bacon makes everything better no matter what the recipe calls for. Since we are The

United States of Bacon we have decided to explore the fifty states in this union of bacon, find the best recipes from each state, and add BACON! That's right! We found the best recipes from each state in the union and added BACON! Sit back in your kitchen and gaze over the recipes within this book and enlighten yourself with the salty sweet goodness that makes this country great! IN BACON WE TRUST!

ALABAMA

SWEET and SALTY BACON FUDGE

INGREDIENTS

- 4 (4-ounce) semisweet chocolate baking bars, chopped
- 1 14-ounce can sweetened condensed milk
- 1/4 cup butter, softened
- 1/4 cup heavy whipping cream
- 1 pound bacon, cooked until crisp
- 2 cups chopped toasted pecans

Line an 8×8-inch baking pan with aluminum foil. Spray with nonstick cooking spray. In a medium saucepan, combine chocolate, condensed milk, butter and cream. Cook over medium-low heat, stirring constantly, until chocolate melts and mixture is smooth. Remove from heat. Crumble bacon, reserving 1/4 cup. Stir pecans and remaining bacon into chocolate mixture. Spoon mixture into prepared pan; smooth top with a spatula. Sprinkle reserved 1/4 cup crumbled bacon over chocolate mixture, pressing down gently. Cover and chill for 4 hours or until set. Cut into squares to serve. Makes about 32 pieces.

BLUE CHEESE, DATE and BACON WRAPS

INGREDIENTS

- 12 bacon strips
- 36 pitted dates
- 2/3 cup crumbled blue cheese

Cut each bacon strip into thirds. In a large skillet, cook bacon in batches over medium heat until partially cooked but not crisp. Remove to paper towels to drain: keep warm. Carefully cut a slit in the center of each date. Fill with blue cheese. Wrap a piece of bacon around each stuffed date. SECURE with wood toothpicks. Place on ungreased baking sheets. Bake in 375 degree oven for 10-12 minutes until bacon is crisp. Yields 3 dozen.

Bacon Fact:

The modern term for a side of bacon is "slab," but before the 12th century, an unsliced slab of bacon was known as a "flitch."

ALASKA

BAKED HALIBUT SUPREME with BACON

Alaska Halibut with bacon, sour cream and parmesan cheese in this baked halibut dish from Great Alaska Seafood

INGREDIENTS

- 3 lbs Halibut Fillets
- 2 tbsp. Butter or margarine
- 1/4 tsp. finely chopped Salt
- dash Pepper
- 1/2 cup Parmesan Cheese, grated
- 4 strips Bacon
- 1 tsp. Lemon Juice
- 1 cup Sour Cream
- 1/3 cup buttered Bread Crumbs
- 1/2 tsp. Parsley fine chop

DIRECTIONS

Rub halibut with butter, salt and pepper. Lay bacon on bottom of baking pan and place fillets of top. Make a mixture of sour cream, cheese, crumbs and lemon juice. Spread over the fish.

Bake halibut at 350F until tender (20 to 30 minutes).

Serve sprinkled with grated cheese and parsley.

Makes 6 - 8 servings.

ALASKA CRAB and BACON WRAPS

INGREDIENTS

- 2 strips of bacon, browned & chopped
- 1 small tomato, chopped (1/2 cup)
- 1 medium green onion, chopped (1 tbsp.)
- ½ lb. crabmeat, cooked & coarsely chopped (King or Dungeness preferably)
- 1 cup iceberg lettuce, finely chopped
- ¼ cup jarred red bell pepper, finely chopped
- 2/3 cup mayonnaise
- 1/8 tsp. hot sauce
- ¼ tsp. garlic powder
- 1/8 tsp. Old Bay Seasoning
- Salt & freshly ground black pepper to taste
- 4 flour tortillas (10")

DIRECTIONS

Cut the bacon strips in half and brown in a small skillet, drain and cool, and then finely chop into bits.

In medium bowl mix all of the ingredients as listed, including the bacon bits, (except not the tortillas).

Heat a large non-stick skillet over medium heat, placing a tortilla into the dry skillet until it slightly bubbles; turn over doing the same—repeat with remaining three tortilla [this process removes its flour and tangy flavor].

Spread 2/3-cup crabmeat mixture on each tortilla; roll up, and then cut diagonally in half, and serve.

Bacon Fact:

A high protein breakfast of bacon and eggs improves the metabolism and facilitates circulation and digestion.

ARIZONA

BACON CINNAMON ROLLS

INGREDIENTS

- 1 can refrigerated cinnamon rolls
- 8 slices pre-cooked bacon

Pre-heat oven to 400. Lightly spray a 9-inch cake pan with cooking spray.

Unwrap the cinnamon rolls and separate into 8 rolls. Unroll each and place a piece of bacon on top of the dough. Gently re-roll. Repeat for remaining rolls. Place the rolls in the cake pan and bake for 15-18 minutes. Remove the rolls from the oven and frost with the glaze that is included with the rolls.

BACON GUACAMOLE

INGREDIENTS

- 1 8-oz pkg bacon
- 2 avocados
- 3 tbsp. cilantro
- 1/4 red onion
- 1 lime
- 2 tsp. Sriracha (optional)

DIRECTIONS

Slice bacon into 1/4-inch strips or cubes and fry to desired doneness.

Halve avocados, remove pits and slice in the skin across the avocado in both directions into 1/4-inch pieces, and then scoop avocado out of skins into a bowl.

Dice red onion into 1/8-inch pieces. Add to bowl.

Chop cilantro. Add to bowl.

Halve lime and squeeze juice over avocado, onion and cilantro.

Add bacon and mix all together. If you want to add a bit of heat, add 1-3 tsps. of Sriracha and mix all together.

Serve with corn chips or use instead of mayo on your next BLT.

Bacon Fact:

Bacon is cured, smoked pork, but different places around the world use different cuts.

ARKANSAS

PEPPERED SAUTE of OZARK with BACON

INGREDIENTS

- Bacon (Mountain Smokehouse)
- Coarsely cracked black peppercorns
- Dark Brown sugar
- Half round slices of Canadian bacon or smoked ham
- Oil Spray

DIRECTIONS

Oil spray a heavy iron skillet and heat over medium heat. With the heel of hand, rub/press peppercorns liberally into one side of Arkansas or Canadian bacon or ham slices. When pan is hot, add bacon/ham, pepper-side down (most of the pepper will fall off; don't worry). Sprinkle top side with additional pepper. Let ham fry in hot skillet until nicely seared and browned, about 2 to 4 minutes, then flip over. Sprinkle the browned side you have just flipped lightly with brown sugar; about 1 tsp per slice. When second side has browned, flip again so the sugared side is directly in contact with the skillet and let sear very quickly 10 to 20 seconds, sprinkling second side with brown sugar. Flip, repeat the quick sear, and remove from the skillet to hot plate. Serve at once. Original recipe makes 1 serving.

ARKANSAS CARBONARA AKS BACON HASH

INGREDIENTS

- 2 strips bacon, diced fairly fine
- 1 small potato, diced about 3/16 to 1/4"
- Salt & pepper to taste
- 35% (Whipping) Cream
- Grated parmesan cheese, to taste (the "Carbonara taste)
- Toasted white or whole-grain bread
- Optional
- A "handful" chopped green onions or minced onion, to taste.
- 2 eggs

DIRECTIONS

1. Fry Bacon bits until done but not completely crisp.
2. Add chopped potato (and minced onion, if desired).
3. Season with salt and pepper to taste.
4. Stir/flip occasionally to get all sides of potato started cooking.
5. Pour off excess fat.
6. Pour in whipping cream to almost cover meat and potatoes.
7. Sprinkle with Parmesan, if desired.
8. If you want, and didn't add onion earlier, add a handful of chopped green onion and stir in.
9. Continue cooking to reduce by about 1/2 to 2/3.
10. Serve over toast.
11. Top or side with fried or scrambled eggs.

Bacon Fact:

Bacon bits sold at the supermarket are actually vegetarian.

CALIFORNIA

CALIFORNIA BACON SUSHI ROLL

INGREDIENTS

- 4 eggs, divided
- 6 tbsp. milk, divided
- 4 tbsp. jack cheese, divided
- cooking spray
- 2 flour tortillas (I used carb balance wheat tortillas)
- 4 strips crisp bacon
- 1/2 large avocado, sliced
- 1/2 large tomato, sliced

  Spicy Sour Cream:
- 2 tbsp. sour cream
- 1 tbsp. sriracha (or other hot sauce)
- 1 tsp. milk

DIRECTIONS

Coat a medium skillet with cooking spray and heat over medium-high heat. In a small bowl whisk 2 eggs and 3 tbsp milk until incorporated. Pour into the hot skillet. Sprinkle with 2 tbsp cheese and cook without stirring for 3-5 minutes, until the top is no longer wet. You may need to turn the heat down so you don't burn the bottom.

Place the tortilla over the egg and gently flip them out on to a cutting board. Place 2 strips of bacon in the bottom 1/4 of the tortilla (closest to you). Top with 1/2 of the sliced avocado and tomato. Roll up as tightly and gently as you can. Allow to rest for a second and then slice with a sharp knife into sushi rolls. Repeat the process with the remaining eggs, cheese, etc.

In a small bowl mix the sour cream, sriracha and milk. Drizzle over the sushi rolls and serve immediately.

CALIFORNIA BACON and EGGS

INGREDIENTS

- Crispy Potato Pancakes
- 4 medium Yukon gold potatoes
- 1/4 cup finely diced onion
- 2 egg whites
- 3 tbsp. rice flour
- Kosher salt and freshly ground black pepper
- Extra-virgin olive oil
- Bacon and Eggs
- 6 slices bacon
- 2 tbsp. extra-virgin olive oil
- 4 eggs
- Celery Pesto
- 2 celery ribs, peeled
- 1/2 cup celery leaves
- 1/2 cup fresh Italian flat-leaf parsley leaves
- 1 garlic clove, peeled and smashed
- 1/4 cup toasted walnuts
- 1/4 cup extra-virgin olive oil
- 2 tbsp. grated Parmigiano-Reggiano
- Kosher salt and freshly ground black pepper

- Celery leaves, for garnish

DIRECTIONS

1.) To prepare Crispy Potato Pancakes, peel and shred potatoes using a mandolin or grater. Place shreds in a kitchen towel and squeeze out any moisture. In a large bowl combine potato, onion, egg whites, and rice flour. Mix well and season with salt and pepper. In a large nonstick skillet heat a 3-count of oil (about 3 tbsp) over medium-high heat. Add spoonfuls of the potato mixture to make free-form cakes about 4 inches in diameter. Fry until golden brown, turning once. Drain on paper towels and season with salt and pepper. Keep warm.

2.) In a saute pan fry bacon over medium-high heat, stirring as it cooks so it curls up. Drain and set aside on paper towels.

3.) In large nonstick skillet heat the 2 tbsp oil over medium heat. Gently add the eggs and fry, sunny-side up, until the yolks are cooked but still runny in the centers. Keep warm.

4.) Just before serving, prepare the Celery Pesto. In a blender combine celery ribs, the 1/2 cup celery leaves, the parsley, garlic, walnuts, and the 1/4 cup olive oil and process until well combined. Add Parmesan and adjust seasoning with salt and pepper.

5.) To assemble, place a spoonful of Celery Pesto on each plate. Top with a Crispy Potato Pancake and a fried egg, sunny-side up. Season with a little salt and pepper. Top with bacon and garnish with celery leaves.

Bacon Fact:
70% of all bacon is the United States is eaten at breakfast time.

COLORADO

LOBSTER COLORADO

INGREDIENTS

- 4 (8 ounce) beef tenderloin filets
- salt and pepper to taste
- 1/2 tsp. garlic powder
- 4 slices bacon
- 1/2 cup butter, divided
- Pinch of bay leaf powder
- Pinch of celery salt
- Pinch of dry mustard
- Pinch of ground black pepper
- Pinch of ground ginger
- Pinch of sweet paprika
- Pinch of white pepper
- Pinch of ground nutmeg
- Pinch of ground cloves
- Pinch of ground allspice
- Pinch of crushed red pepper
- Pinch of ground mace
- Pinch of ground cardamom
- Pinch of ground cinnamon
- 8 ounces lobster tail, cleaned and chopped

DIRECTIONS

Set oven to Broil at 500 degrees F (260 degrees C).

Sprinkle tenderloins all over with salt, pepper, and garlic powder. Wrap each filet with bacon, and secure with a toothpick. Place on a broiling pan, and broil to desired doneness, about 8 to 10 minutes per side for medium rare.

Place all the pinches in a small bowl and mix together to form a seafood seasoning. While tenderloins are cooking, melt 1/4 cup of butter over medium heat with 1/2 tsp of seafood seasoning. Stir in chopped lobster meat, and cook until done. Spoon lobster meat over cooked tenderloins, and return them to the broiler until the lobster meat begins to brown.

While the lobster is in the oven, heat the remaining 1/4 cup of butter in a small saucepan over medium-high heat, cook until it browns, turning the color of a hazelnut. To serve, spoon the browned butter over the steaks, and sprinkle with the remaining seafood seasoning.

COLORADO CORN and BACON SALSA

INGREDIENTS

- 5 ears Colorado sweet corn
- 5 tbsp. butter, melted
- kosher or sea salt, to taste
- freshly ground black pepper, to taste
- 1 red onion
- 3 fresno peppers or red jalapenos
- 12 strips thick cut bacon
- 1 tbsp. garlic puree
- 1/2 cup pinto beans, rinsed
- 1/2 cup black beans, rinsed

- 1 cup tomato sauce
- 2 tsps. cumin
- 1 tbsp. dark chili powder
- fresh lime Juice to taste
- 5 tbsp. fresh cilantro, chopped, no stems

DIRECTIONS

Peel the husk back on the corn, do not tear off, and remove the silk. Brush each ear of corn with melted butter and season with the salt and pepper. Replace the husk on the corn. On medium heat on outdoor grill, grill the corn with the husk on until tender. Remove the husk and continue grilling until the corn starts to show grill marks, then remove from the heat and allow to cool. Cook the peppers on the grill until well roasted, remove, cool and dice. Split the red onion in half, brush with butter and season with salt and pepper. Grill both halves of the red onion until well-cooked then remove, cool and dice. Cook the bacon in a skillet until fully cooked then remove, cool and chop. Once the corn is cooled, trim the niblets from the ear and place into a large bowl. Add the remaining ingredients, except the bacon, lime juice and cilantro. Mix well and season to taste then add the lime juice and cilantro and mix well. Add the bacon and mix. Taste and adjust seasoning as needed. This recipe goes great with grilled flour tortillas, white corn tortilla chips or as a side for any grilled meat. Makes 8 to 10 servings.

Bacon Fact:

The term, "To bring home the bacon" comes from the ancient sport of catching a greased pig at country fairs. The winner kept the pig and 'brought' home the bacon'.

CONNECTICUT

CONNECTICUT BACON and SPINACH SALAD

INGREDIENTS

- 8 oz. sliced bacon
- 1/3 cup red wine vinegar
- 2 tbsp. sugar
- 1 tsp. dry mustard
- 1 lb. fresh spinach, stemmed, washed, dried & torn into bite-size pieces
- 2 1/2 cups sliced fresh mushrooms
- 1 small red onion, thinly sliced
- 2 hard cooked eggs, coarsely chopped

DIRECTIONS

Fry bacon in 12 inch skillet over medium heat, turning occasionally until crisp. Remove bacon to paper towels to drain, then crumble and reserve. Pour off and discard all but 2 tbsp bacon fat. Stir vinegar, sugar, mustard and 1/4 cup water into bacon fat in skillet and bring to boil. Simmer 5 minutes, stirring occasionally.

Combine spinach, mushrooms and onion in large bowl. Sprinkle crumbled bacon and eggs on top. Serve salad tossed with dressing. 4-6 servings.

DOUBLE ONION BACON BURGER

INGREDIENTS
- 1 lb. ground sirloin
- ½ cup grated white onion
- 2 tbsp. BBQ sauce, plus more for topping
- 1 tbsp. each Kosher salt and pepper
- 4 slices extra sharp cheddar cheese
- 6 sliced thick cut bacon, cooked crisp
- 4 onion rolls, sliced
- Iceberg lettuce and sliced tomato (optional)

DIRECTIONS

Add sirloin, grated onions, BBQ sauce, and salt and pepper to a bowl. Mix well with hands to combine. Divide into 4 patties and set aside. Heat grill to medium high and cook burgers for 4 minutes per side for medium rare, adding sliced cheese once you've turned the burger. Remove from heat and tent with foil. Assemble burger by adding bacon, a handful of frizzled onions, a piece of lettuce, and an extra slathering of BBQ sauce.

The Frizzled Onions:

- 1 whole large onion
- 2 cups buttermilk
- 2 cups all-purpose flour
- 1 tbsp. kosher salt
- 1/4 tsp. cayenne pepper
- 1 quart canola oil
- Black pepper

Slice onion very thin. Place in a baking dish, cover with buttermilk and soak for at least an hour. Combine dry ingredients and set aside. Heat oil in a deep pot to 375 degrees.

Add small batches of onions, to the flour mixture, tap to shake off excess, and plunge into hot oil. Fry for a few minutes and remove as soon as golden brown. Repeat until onions are cooked.

Bacon Fact:

The BLT (Bacon, Lettuce, & Tomato) sandwiches became popular after World War II, when supermarkets expanded, making fresh lettuce and tomatoes available year round.

DELAWARE

DELAWARE CREAMED BACON SUCCOTASH

INGREDIENTS

- 2 1/2 cups fresh lima beans
- 6 strips bacon, diced
- 2 large onions, finely chopped
- 2 1/2 cups fresh corn kernels (plus milk scraped from the cobs)
- 2 cups peeled and chopped ripe tomatoes, juices included
- 3/4 cup half-and-half
- 1/8 tsp. ground nutmeg
- Salt and freshly ground black pepper, to taste
- Store-bought or homemade Tabasco sauce, to taste

DIRECTIONS

1. Place the lima beans in a medium saucepan with enough salted water to cover, bring to a moderate simmer, cover, cook till tender, about 15 minutes, and drain.

2. Meanwhile, in a large, heavy pot, fry the bacon over moderate heat till almost crisp and pour off all but about 3 tbsp of the bacon grease.

3. Add the onions and stir till softened, about 2 minutes. Add the lima beans, the corn plus the milk from the cobs, the tomatoes and their juices, and the half-and-half, stir well, and continue to cook another 5 minutes. Season the succotash with nutmeg, salt and pepper, and Tabasco and continue to cook, stirring carefully to prevent sticking, till the succotash has thickened slightly.

4. Transfer the succotash to an earthenware tureen or deep serving dish and serve hot.

BACON-WRAPPED SEAFOOD SKEWERS

INGREDIENTS

- 2 tbsp. lemon juice
- 1/2 tsp. cayenne pepper
- 1/8 tsp. garlic powder
- 12 uncooked jumbo shrimp, peeled and deveined
- 6 large sea scallops, halved widthwise
- 12 bacon strips, halved
- 1 medium lemon, cut into wedges

DIRECTIONS

In a large resealable plastic bag, combine the lemon juice, cayenne and garlic powder; add shrimp and scallops. Seal bag and turn to coat; let stand for 10 minutes.

Meanwhile, in a large skillet, cook bacon over medium heat until partially cooked but not crisp. Drain on paper towels. Drain and discard marinade. Wrap one bacon piece around each shrimp and scallop half.

On six metal or soaked wooden skewers, alternately thread the shrimp, scallops and lemon wedges. Grill, covered, over medium heat for 8-12 minutes or until shrimp turn pink and scallops are opaque, turning occasionally. Remove from skewers; squeeze lemon wedges over seafood. Yield: 3 servings.

Bacon Fact:
Bacon comes from the belly of the pig.

FLORIDA

CREAMY BACON-MUSHROOM SHRIMP and GRITS

INGREDIENTS

- 1 pound medium shrimp, peeled and deveined
- grits for 4 servings
- 3 slices bacon, chopped
- 2 tbsp. olive oil
- 1 small onion, finely minced
- 1 large clove garlic, minced
- 1/3 cup celery, chopped fine
- 1/3 cup green pepper, chopped fine
- 1 sprig fresh thyme
- 1 bay leaf
- 1 cup mushrooms, sliced
- 1 cup half-and-half
- 1/2 tsp. ground cayenne pepper
- Dash hot pepper sauce
- 2 tsps. fresh lemon juice
- parsley, chopped

DIRECTIONS

Prepare grits according to package directions; set aside and keep warm.

Fry bacon until crisp then remove from pan and set aside.

Pour off all but 1 tbsp of fat in the pan and add olive oil to bacon fat; heat over medium-high heat.

Add onion, garlic, celery, green pepper, thyme, bay leaf and mushrooms; sauté until soft.

Add shrimp and cook until pink and cooked through.

Stir in cream, bacon, cayenne pepper, hot sauce and lemon juice; simmer until heated through.

In individual bowls or plates, spoon shrimp over grits; sprinkle with parsley and serve.

SPICY JALAPENO BACON & CHEESE OYSTERS

INGREDIENTS

- 36 oysters, shucked, on the half shell
- Rock salt
- 12 ounces mozzarella cheese, grated
- ½ cup cooked bacon, crumbled
- 4 jalapeno peppers, chopped

DIRECTIONS

Arrange oysters on rock salt in a baking dish.

Top each oyster with ½ tsp. of cheese crumbled bacon and chopped jalapeno to taste.

Bake in a preheated oven at 350 degrees for 10 minutes or until edges of oysters begin to curl.

Bacon Fact:

Bacon is one of the oldest processed meats in history. The Chinese began salting pork bellies as early as 1500 B.C.

GEORGIA

GEORGIA BACON PEACH BURGER

INGREDIENTS

- 2 lbs. well marbled chuck
- 1 tsp. kosher salt
- 3 tbsp. light white wine
- 3 cups shredded cabbage and carrots or pre-made coleslaw cabbage
- 1/3 cup Peach Preserves
- 3 tbsp. Dijon mustard
- 9 slices crisp cooked bacon
- 6 slices (large enough to fit on a bun) sharp cheddar cheese
- 6 Kaiser or seeded burger buns

DIRECTIONS

Prepare a medium-hot fire in a charcoal grill with a cover, or preheat a gas grill to medium-high.

To make the patties, cut the Chuck into 3/4 cubes. Place into a food processor, a couple of handfuls at a time. Use the pulse feature and chop for just a moment 10-12 times. Add a pinch of the salt and a tbsp of the wine each time. Repeat until the chunks are all chopped. (If you do not have a food processor just use ground Chuck from your grocer. Handling the meat as little as possible to avoid compacting it, divide the mixture into 5oz portions and form the portions into patties to fit the rolls.

Next, mix the Peach preserves and Mustard together and add to the cabbage mixture. Set aside in the refrigerator.

Heat a pan on the grill or the stove and cook the bacon strips until crispy. Drain and set aside.

When the grill is ready, brush the grill rack with vegetable oil, place the patties on the rack, cover, and cook, turning once, until done to preference, 5 minutes on each side for medium. Place a slice of the cheese on the patties to melt when almost done. During the last few minutes of cooking, place the rolls, cut side down, on the outer edges of the rack to toast lightly.

To assemble the burgers: On each roll bottom, place a patty, and top with 2 slices of bacon. Place a generous spoonful of the Peach/Mustard Slaw on top. Add the roll tops and serve. Makes 6 burgers.

BACON-PEACH COBBLER

INGREDIENTS
- 3 lbs. Peaches, sliced
- 3 Thick Slices of Bacon
- Pinch Salt
- Pinch Cinnamon
- 1 cup Nitrate free Raisins
- 1 cup Chopped Pecans

DIRECTIONS

Heat a pot over medium high heat. Chop the bacon into bits, and then brown in a little coconut oil in the pot. Add the salt and cinnamon and cook for a minute longer.

Reduce the heat to medium-low and add the peaches. Stir until well combined and the peaches are nicely coated in cinnamon-y bacon grease. Reduce heat to low, then cover the pot and let simmer for 1 hour.

Add the raisins and pecans and cook for 10-15 minutes, or until raisins are plumped. Remove from heat, cool slightly and serve.

Bacon Fact:

Most popular bacon flavors: Hickory, Maple, Applewood, Mesquite, Honey, Sugared, and Peppered.

HAWAII

HAWAIIAN BBQ BACON CHEESEBURGER

INGREDIENTS

- 3 lbs Peaches, sliced
- 3 Thick Slices of Bacon
- Pinch Salt
- Pinch Cinnamon
- 1 cup Nitrate free Raisins
- 1 cup Chopped Pecans
- 1 pound ground beef
- Salt/Pepper
- ½ cup BBQ Sauce
- 6 slices bacon, cooked
- 4 slices Cheese (Velveeta, Cheddar, American, or Swiss)
- 1 (8oz.) can pineapple slices in pineapple juice (contains 4 slices)

DIRECTIONS

Mold ground beef into four burger patties and sprinkle lightly with salt and pepper

Cook on grill or stovetop until it's nearly reached your desired level of doneness. About halfway through, add your pineapple to the grill. Flip the pineapple once the bottom begins to char.

Brush each burger generously with BBQ Sauce. Top with bacon slices, cheese, and pineapple.

HAWAIIAN BACON PIZZA

INGREDIENTS

Crust:

1 premade pizza crust.

Toppings:
- 4 slices center-cut bacon
- 3/4 cup (6 ounces) shredded part-skim mozzarella
- 1/4 cup diced red onion
- 1 cup pineapple chunks (fresh or canned, drained)

Sauce:
- 4 Roma tomatoes, peeled, seeded and cored
- 1/2 tsp. Italian seasoning
- 1/2 tsp. basil
- 1/2 tsp. fennel seed
- 1/2 tsp. salt
- 1/2 tsp. red pepper flakes
- 1/2 tbsp. extra virgin olive oil
- 1/4 tsp. minced garlic
- 1 tsp. brown sugar (unpacked)

DIRECTIONS

Set a large frying pan over medium heat, spritz with nonstick cooking spray and add bacon. Cook bacon for eight minutes, flipping every two minutes to keep it from curling up. Place bacon on paper towels to drain. The bacon should still be flexible and soft; it will crisp up on the pizza. Tear into small pieces.

Place tomatoes in a blender along with all the spices, salt, sugar and oil. Blend till smooth and pour into pot. Cook on medium high for 30 minutes or until reduced by half.

While the tomato sauce is cooking, dice the onions and drain the pineapple.

Roll out the dough into your desired shape and thickness. Place on a baking sheet lined with aluminum foil and sprayed with cooking spray. Preheat the oven to 425 degrees Fahrenheit.

Place 1/2 cup of sauce on pizza. Sprinkle on 1/2 cup of cheese, 1 cup of pineapple and bacon pieces. Sprinkle on remaining 1/4 cup of cheese.

Bake in oven for 14 minutes on middle rack. If you prefer a browner pizza, broil pizza for an additional couple of minutes, watching to ensure it doesn't burn. Once it looks good and brown remove and let sit for 10 minutes to let the cheese firm up a little. Slice into eight pieces.

Bacon Fact:

Yorkshire and Tamworth pigs are bred specifically for bacon.

IDAHO

BACON CHEDDAR MASHED POTATOES

INGREDIENTS

- 8 servings Instant Mashed Idaho Potatoes-prepared
- 10 oz. Mild Cheddar Cheese-shredded
- 8 oz. Bacon-diced, fully cooked
- ¼ cup Parsley-fresh, chopped
- ¼ tsp. White Pepper

DIRECTIONS

Prepare Instant Mashed Idaho Potatoes, fully cooked and drain bacon, shred cheddar cheese. Mix ingredients thoroughly. Bake at 350° F for 15 minutes, covered.

IDAHO BACON BURGERS

INGREDIENTS

- 1 1/2 lbs Lean Ground beef
- 1 cup Cornflakes
- 1/2 cup Barbecue Sauce (your favorite)
- 1 Onion, chopped
- 6 Slices of Bacon
- 1 tsp. Garlic Salt
- 1/2 tsp. Red Pepper

DIRECTIONS

Combine all ingredients except the bacon and shape into 6 patties about 3/4" thick. Wrap a slice of Bacon around each patty and fasten with a toothpick. Lay into a 6-up hamburger basket and grill until cooked thoroughly. Be sure to remove the toothpicks before serving.

Now if you do not have a grill basket you can use aluminum foil. Put the shiny side in and then do not use the toothpick to hold the bacon. In about 4 minutes turn the foil over and then in about 3 minutes check to see if it is done. Depending on how you like them they might be done. Use good hot pads or leather gloves to take it off the fire. This is really HOT!

Bacon Fact:

More than 2 billion pounds of bacon are produced in the U.S. each year.

ILLINOIS

PIZZA with CARAMELIZED ONIONS and CRISPY BACON

INGREDIENTS

- 1 tsp. olive oil
- 3 slices bacon (about 2 ounces), cut into 1/2-inch pieces
- 1 small onion, peeled, thinly sliced
- 2 tbsp. mascarpone cheese
- 1/4 cup farmer's cheese
- Freshly grated nutmeg
- Freshly ground black pepper
- 6 ounces Pizza Dough, recipe follows
- 1/2 cup grated mozzarella
- 2 tbsp. grated Parmesan
- 2 tbsp. fresh thyme leaves

Pizza Dough:

- 1 package active dry or fresh yeast
- 1 tsp. honey
- 1 cup warm water, 105 to 115 degrees F
- 3 cups all-purpose flour
- 1 tsp. kosher salt
- 1 tbsp. extra-virgin olive oil, plus additional for brushing

DIRECTIONS

Place a pizza stone on the middle rack of the oven and preheat the oven to 500 degrees F.

In a medium size saute pan, add olive oil and heat over medium heat. When the oil is hot, add the bacon and cook until the bacon is very crispy and all of the fat is rendered. Remove the bacon with a slotted spoon and drain on a paper towel-lined plate. Remove all but 2 tbsp of the bacon fat from the pan and discard. Place the pan over high heat. Add the onions to the hot bacon fat and cook until the onions are well browned, about 8 to 10 minutes, stirring often. Remove to a paper towel lined plate.

In a small bowl, combine the mascarpone and farmer's cheeses. Season with nutmeg and black pepper. Reserve.

On a lightly floured surface, stretch or roll the dough as thinly as possible, about 14 to 15-inch circle. Evenly spread the mascarpone mixture over the dough. Sprinkle with the mozzarella and Parmesan cheeses, bacon, thyme, and sautéed onion. Bake until the pizza crust is nicely browned, about 8 to 10 minutes.

Remove pizza from the oven, transfer to a cutting board, cut into slices and serve immediately.

Pizza Dough:

In a small bowl, dissolve the yeast and honey in 1/4 cup warm water.

In a food processor, combine the flour and the salt. Add the oil, the yeast mixture, and the remaining 3/4 cup of water and process until the mixture forms a ball. (The pizza dough can also be made in a mixer fitted with a dough hook. Mix on low speed until the mixture comes cleanly away from the sides of the bowl and starts to climb up the dough hook).

Turn the dough out onto a clean work surface and knead by hand 2 or 3 minutes longer. The dough should be smooth and firm. Cover the dough with a clean, damp towel and let it rise in a cool spot for about 2 hours. (When ready, the dough will stretch as it is lightly pulled).

Divide the dough into 4 balls, about 6 ounces each. Work each ball by pulling down the sides and tucking under the bottom of the ball. Repeat 4 or 5 times. Then on a smooth, unfloured surface, roll the ball under the palm of your hand until the top of the dough is smooth and firm, about 1 minute. Cover the dough with a damp towel and let rest 1 hour. At this point, the balls can be wrapped in plastic and refrigerated for up to 2 days.

CHICAGO BACON DOG

INGREDIENTS
- 1 all-beef hot dog
- 1 poppyseed hot dog bun
- 1 tbsp. sweet neon green pickle relish
- 1 tbsp. chopped onion
- 4 tomato wedges
- 1 dill pickle spear
- 2 sport peppers
- 1 dash celery salt
- 1 or 2 strips of maple bacon

Bring a pot of water to a boil. Reduce heat to low, place hot dog in water, and cook 5 minutes or until done. Remove hot dog and set aside. Carefully place a steamer basket into the pot and steam the hot dog bun 2 minutes or until warm.

Place hot dog in the steamed bun. Pile on the toppings in this order: yellow mustard, sweet neon green pickle relish, onion, tomato wedges, pickle spear, bacon, sport peppers, and celery salt. The tomatoes should be nestled between the hot dog and the top of the bun. Place the pickle between the hot dog and the bottom of the bun. Place bacon on top with peppers on the very top. No ketchup!

Bacon Fact:
In the 16th Century European peasants would proudly display the small amount of bacon they could afford.

INDIANA

BACON-WRAPPED SHRIMP with BBQ SAUCE

INGREDIENTS
- 12 strips of applewood smoked bacon
- 12 fresh gulf shrimp, peeled and de-veined (16-20 count)
- 1 cup of your favorite BBQ sauce with a dash of Tabasco
- 12 long round toothpicks

DIRECTIONS

Pan fry bacon until halfway cooked, so it is still easily pliable. Place bacon on paper towels to drain and cool. Grill or pan fry shrimp for 2-3 minutes, place the shrimp on a plate and cool slightly.

Next, wrap the bacon around the shrimp so it wraps around twice, push toothpick through the bacon and shrimp to secure.

Finally, cook the bacon-wrapped shrimp either on a grill or in a fry pan for another 1-2 minutes, so bacon becomes crisp.

Serve shrimp on a festive plate, brush with spicy BBQ sauce and serve warm!

MAPLE BACON MONKEY BREAD

INGREDIENTS

- cooking spray
- 1 (12 ounce) package bacon
- 1/2 cup margarine
- 3/4 cup packed dark brown sugar
- 1/2 cup maple syrup
- 3/4 cup white sugar
- 2 tsps. ground cinnamon
- 2 (16.3 ounce) packages refrigerated biscuit dough, separated and cut into quarters

DIRECTIONS

Preheat oven to 350 degrees F (175 degrees C). Coat the inside of a 9-inch fluted tube pan (such as Bundt®) with cooking spray.

Place bacon in a large skillet and cook over medium-high heat, turning occasionally, until evenly browned, about 10 minutes. Drain the bacon slices on paper towels; crumble and remove extra fat.

Melt margarine in a small saucepan over medium heat; stir in brown sugar and maple syrup. Bring mixture to a boil; cook and stir until mixture begins to foam, about 1 minute. Remove saucepan from heat.

Mix white sugar and cinnamon in a resealable plastic bag; add 6 to 8 biscuit pieces at a time and shake until well coated. Pour any remaining sugar-cinnamon mixture into brown sugar mixture. Place saucepan over medium heat and cook and stir until sugar dissolves, 2 to 3 minutes.

Sprinkle 1/4 the bacon pieces in the bottom of the tube pan; pour in about 1/4 the brown sugar mixture. Arrange 1 layer of biscuit pieces in the tube pan; sprinkle in 1/4 the bacon pieces. Drizzle about 1/4 the brown sugar mixture over the biscuit pieces. Continue layering until all the ingredients are used, ending with a drizzle of brown sugar mixture.

Bake in the preheated oven until biscuits are cooked through, about 35 minutes. Allow to cool in pan, 10 to 20 minutes; invert onto a serving plate.

Bacon Fact:
One 200 lb. pig will produce approximately 20 lbs. of bacon.

IOWA

IOWA BACON CORN CHOWDER

INGREDIENTS

- 3 slices bacon, diced
- 1 lb. boned chicken breasts, cut into cubes
- 3/4 cup finely chopped onions
- 3/4 cup finely chopped celery
- 4 cups chicken broth
- 4 cups whole kernel corn
- 2 cups diced potatoes
- 1/2 tsp. salt
- 1 cup heavy whipping cream
- 2 tbsp. chopped parsley
- 1/8 tsp. white pepper

DIRECTIONS

Over medium heat, cook bacon until crisp. Pour off all but 2 tbsp of grease. Add chicken, onion and celery; cook 10-15 minutes. In blender on high, put 1 cup chicken broth and 2 cups corn. Blend on high until smooth.

In pot, stir pureed corn and remaining kernels, potatoes, chicken broth and salt. Bring to a boil over high heat, reduce heat and simmer partly covered for 20 minutes until potatoes are tender. Stir in cream, parsley and pepper. Simmer another 2 or 3 minutes and stir in bacon. Serves 6.

BACON and BAKED POTATO SOUP

INGREDIENTS

- 2 6 - 8 - ounces baking potatoes (such as russet or Yukon gold)
- 3 tbsp. butter
- 1/2 cup chopped onion
- 1/4 cup chopped celery
- 3 tbsp. all-purpose flour
- 1/2 tsp. dried thyme, crushed
- 1/4 tsp. salt
- 1/8 tsp. ground black pepper
- 4 cups half-and-half, light cream or milk
- 1 1/4 cups shredded American cheese (5 ounces)
- 1 cup chicken broth
- 8 slices bacon, crisp-cooked, drained and crumbled
- 2 tbsp. thinly sliced green onion
- 1/4 cup dairy sour cream

DIRECTIONS

Scrub potatoes with a vegetable brush; pat dry. Prick potatoes with a fork. Bake in a 425 degree F oven for 40 to 60 minutes or until tender; cool. Peel potatoes (if desired) and chop potatoes; set aside.

In a heavy large saucepan or Dutch oven, melt butter over medium heat. Add onion and celery. Cook and stir about 5 minutes or until crisp-tender. Stir in flour, thyme, salt and pepper. Add half-and-half or milk all at once. Cook and stir for 5 to 6 minutes or until thickened and bubbly. Add potatoes, 1 cup of the cheese, and the broth; stir until cheese melts. Slightly mash potatoes with the back of a spoon or a potato masher.

For the topping, reserve 2 tbsps. of the bacon. Stir the remaining bacon and 1 tbsp. of the green onion into soup. Heat through.

To serve, top each serving with reserved bacon, remaining 1/4 cup cheese, green onions and the sour cream. Makes 6 servings (about 1 cup each).

Bacon Fact:

The earliest reference of bacon was in 1560 by a London Cheesemonger.

KANSAS

BARBEQUE BACON CHICKEN BAKE

INGREDIENTS

- cooking spray
- 8 slices bacon
- 4 skinless, boneless chicken breast halves
- 3/4 cup barbeque sauce (your choice)

DIRECTIONS

Preheat oven to 350 degrees F (175 degrees C). Spray a 9x13-inch baking dish with cooking spray.

Cook bacon in a skillet over medium heat until the edges begin to crisp, about 5 minutes; drain bacon on paper towels. Wrap each chicken breast with 2 slices of bacon in an x-shaped pattern and place into the prepared baking sheet with bacon ends underneath.

Bake in the preheated oven for 30 minutes; spread barbeque sauce over chicken breasts and bake until the juices run clear, the chicken is no longer pink inside, and an instant-read meat thermometer inserted into the thickest part of a breast reads at least 160 degrees F (70 degrees C), 10 to 15 more minutes.

APPLE-BACON BARBEQUE SAUCE

INGREDIENTS

- 1/4 lb. (4 to 5 slices) bacon
- 3/4 cup apple juice
- 5 tbsp. apple cider vinegar
- 1/2 cup ketchup
- 2 tsp. Worcestershire sauce
- 1/2 tsp. ancho chile powder
- 1/2 tsp. sweet paprika, preferably Hungarian
- 1/4 tsp. ground cumin
- 1/4 tsp. celery seed
- 1/4 tsp. freshly ground black pepper

DIRECTIONS

Cook the bacon in a medium skillet over medium-low heat until browned and crisp, 10 to 15 minutes, turning occasionally. Drain the bacon on paper towels and eat it whenever you like. Pour about one-half the bacon fat into a small saucepan and reserve the remaining fat in the skillet for the barbecue sauce. To the saucepan, add 1/2 cup of the apple juice and 2 tbsp. of the cider vinegar. Bring to a simmer over medium heat and then remove from the heat (this is the mop).

Add the remaining 1/4 cup apple juice, 3 tbsp. cider vinegar, and the ketchup, Worcestershire sauce, chile powder, paprika, cumin, celery seed, and pepper to the bacon fat in the skillet. Cook over medium-low heat, whisking until smooth. As soon as the barbecue sauce simmers, remove the skillet from the heat.

Bacon Fact:

The Chicago Mercantile Exchange has traded pork bellies since 1961.

KENTUCKY

OLD TIME KENTUCKY BACON MILK GRAVY for BISCUITS

INGREDIENTS

- 1/4 cup bacon drippings
- 1/4 cup all-purpose flour
- 1 tsp. salt, or to taste
- 1 tsp. ground black pepper, or to taste
- 4 cups milk, divided

DIRECTIONS

Heat bacon drippings in a skillet over medium heat; whisk flour into drippings until smooth. Reduce heat to low and cook the flour mixture until it turns a caramel brown color, stirring constantly, about 15 minutes. Be careful, the roux burns easily. Stir in salt and black pepper.

Whisk 1/2 cup milk into the roux until thoroughly blended. Continue whisking milk into the gravy, 1/2 cup at a time, whisking in each amount of milk completely before adding more. Bring gravy to a simmer and whisk constantly until thick, smooth, and bubbling.

BACON MAC and CHEESE

INGREDIENTS

- 1 lb. elbow macaroni or other short pasta
- 2 tbsps. olive oil, plus more for the baking dish
- 2 leeks, cut into 1/2-inch thick half-moons
- Kosher salt
- Pepper
- 1 clove garlic, finely chopped
- 1 tbsp. all-purpose flour
- 1 1/2 cups whole milk
- 4 ounces low-fat cream cheese
- 1/4 tsp. freshly grated or ground nutmeg
- 1/8 tsp. cayenne
- 8 ounces (1 cup) extra-sharp Cheddar, shredded
- 8 ounces (1 cup) Gruyère, shredded
- 6 slices bacon
- 1 cup fresh bread crumbs
- 1/2 cups chopped flat-leaf parsley

DIRECTIONS

Heat oven to 425 degrees F. Oil a shallow 3-quart baking dish or six 2-cup ramekins. Cook the pasta according to package directions.

Meanwhile, heat 1 tbsp of the oil in a large skillet over medium-low heat. Add the leeks, 3/4 tsp salt, and 1/4 tsp pepper and cook, covered, stirring occasionally, until very tender, 8 to 10 minutes. Stir in the garlic and cook for 1 minute. Sprinkle the flour over the leek mixture and cook, stirring constantly, for 1 minute.

Whisk in the milk and bring to a simmer. Whisk in the cream cheese, nutmeg, and cayenne until blended. Stir in the Cheddar and Gruyère and simmer, stirring occasionally, until cheese is melted and the mixture has slightly thickened, 1 to 2 minutes.

Toss the pasta with the cheese sauce and transfer to the prepared baking dish. Cook the bacon in a skillet over medium heat until crisp, about 5 minutes. Transfer to a paper towel–lined plate; crumble when cool.

In a small bowl, toss the bacon, bread crumbs, parsley, the remaining 1 tbsp. olive oil, and 1/4 tsp each salt and pepper. Sprinkle over the macaroni and cheese and bake until golden brown, 10 to 12 minutes.

Bacon Fact:
Thin sliced is 1/32 inch thick. (28-32 slices/lb.)

LOUISIANA

BACON JAMBALAYA

INGREDIENTS

- 6 slices bacon, cut into 1 inch pieces
- 1 cup chopped celery
- 1 green bell pepper, seeded and chopped
- 1 onion, chopped
- 1/2 pound cubed cooked ham
- 1/2 pound cubed cooked chicken
- 1/2 pound cubed smoked sausage
- 2 (14.5 ounce) cans crushed tomatoes, with liquid
- 2 cups beef broth
- 2 cups chicken broth
- 1 tsp. dried thyme
- 2 tsps. Cajun seasoning
- 2 cups uncooked white rice
- 1/2 pound salad shrimp

DIRECTIONS

Heat a large pot over medium-high heat. Add bacon, and cook until crisp. Remove bacon pieces with a slotted spoon, and set aside. Add celery, bell pepper, and onion to the bacon drippings, and cook until tender.

Add the ham, chicken and sausage to the pot, and pour in the tomatoes, beef broth and chicken broth. Season with thyme and Cajun seasoning. Bring to a boil, and add the rice. Bring to a boil, then turn the heat to low, cover, and simmer for about 20 minutes, until the rice is tender.

Stir in the shrimp and bacon just before serving, and heat through. If you use uncooked shrimp, let it cook for about 5 minutes before serving.

HOT BACON SALAD DRESSING

INGREDIENTS

- 10 slices smoked lean bacon
- 2 tsps. brown sugar
- 1/2 cup red wine vinegar
- 1/2 tsp. prepared horseradish
- 1/4 tsp. black pepper
- 10 green onions, chopped
- 1 egg yolk, boiled and grated
- Salt and pepper, to taste (optional)

DIRECTIONS

In a skillet, sauté bacon until crisp; crumble into pan. Drain, reserving a tbsp. of bacon drippings. Add sugar, vinegar, horseradish and pepper.

Chop green onions (use the green tops as well as the white positions). Sauté for 1 minute.

Pour immediately over baby lettuce or potatoes. Sprinkle boiled, grated egg over the salad as a garnish.

Note: Be sure lettuce or potatoes are dry so they are better able to absorb the dressing.

Season, if desired, with salt and pepper. Serve hot.

Bacon Fact:

Bacon is addictive. It contains 6 types of umami. Umami produces an addictive neurochemical response.

MAINE

MAPLE PECAN BACON BAKED BRIE

INGREDIENTS

- 1 (16-ounce) wheel of Brie
- 1/2 cup (1 stick) unsalted butter
- 2 tbsp. packed brown sugar
- 1/3 cup pure maple syrup
- 1 cup toasted and chopped pecans
- 1 tsp. coarsely ground black pepper
- Crackers, to serve

DIRECTIONS

Preheat oven to 350 degrees.

Shave off the top rind of the Brie (it is easiest to do this after it has been in the freezer for about 20 minutes). If the Brie came in a wooden box, return it to the original container. If not, create a makeshift "box" out of a few layers of aluminum foil, leaving the top of the Brie exposed.

Place the cheese on a rimmed baking sheet. Bake until warm and gooey, 15 to 20 minutes. Remove from the oven and allow to cool for 20 minutes before serving. Carefully transfer to a serving platter; you do not want the rind to puncture, if possible.

While the Brie is cooling, make the praline sauce. Melt the butter in a saucepan over medium heat. Add the brown sugar, maple syrup, and pecans. Cook, stirring constantly, until all of the ingredients are well combined, 3 to 5 minutes. Stir in coarsely ground black pepper and remove from heat. Allow the mixture to cool for 5 to 10 minutes, until it has thickened up just a bit. Dollop the warm sauce over the baked cheese. (There may be extra praline sauce.) Serve with assorted crackers.

Cook's Note: The praline sauce can be made the day before. To reheat, microwave in increments of 20 seconds, or heat in a small saucepan over medium-low heat until warm.

BACON WRAPPED LOBSTER

Crisp bacon and buttery lobster are a dream combination.

Yield: 16 – 20 lobster bites

INGREDIENTS

- 1 pound cooked lobster meat in chunks
- 8 – 10 slices bacon, slices cut in half (resulting in pieces about 1" x 4")
- 3 scallions, cut into 3" pieces, and sliced into quarters lengthwise
- Freshly ground black pepper
- ½ lemon
- Maple syrup to drizzle

DIRECTIONS

Preheat the broiler to high. Pair each chunk of lobster with a scallion slice, and wrap in a piece of bacon. Hold in form with a toothpick. Place on a baking tray and repeat with other chunks of lobster. Broil for 6 minutes on the 2nd shelf down from the top, turning once, or until bacon begins to crisp.

Arrange bacon-wrapped lobster on a serving platter, drizzle with lemon and maple syrup, and serve with plenty of napkins!

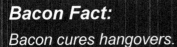

Bacon Fact:

Bacon cures hangovers.

MARYLAND

MARYLAND BACON CRAB SOUP

INGREDIENTS

- 1 dozen well-seasoned Maryland Steamed Crabs
- 3 lbs. mixed frozen vegetables
- 2 lbs. frozen corn
- 2 lbs. frozen string beans
- bay leaves
- Old bay Seasoning
- Oregano
- 1 16 oz. can tomato sauce
- A few cans tomato paste
- 1 lb. fresh bacon
- Sea salt

DIRECTIONS

Place the crabs in a large pot

Add enough water to completely cover the crabs.

Bring the water to a boil and boil the crabs for 15 to 20 minutes. You will know when they are done because they will be bright orange.

While the crabs are boiling, cut the bacon into 1 inch pieces and cook in a separate pan.

When the crabs are done, remove the crabs from the pot and place them aside to cool. Tip: They will cool faster if you go ahead and break them open.

Add the tomato sauce and 3 cans of water to the pot.

Add the frozen mixed vegetable, frozen corn, and frozen string beans to the pot.

Toss in the Old Bay Seasoning, a couple of bay leaves, and a couple of dashes of oregano.

Add the crabs back to the pot and add the bacon as well.

Simmer on low for 2 to 3 hours.

Add the tomato paste to the soup to help thicken it up some. How much you will need depends on how think you like it. It should not be very thick, but you definitely want it to be a little thicker than water.

Add the potatoes to the soup and let it cook until the potatoes are soft.

Taste the soup and add more Old Bay Seasoning and sea salt to taste.

Ladle into bowl and enjoy!

BACON DOUBLE FRIED CHICKEN

INGREDIENTS
- Fried Chicken
- 1 fryer chicken, cut up
- juice of 1 lemon
- 1 tsp. garlic salt
- 3/4 cup all-purpose flour
- 3/4 cup bread Crumbs
- 1 tbsp. paprika
- 2 tsp. salt
- 1 tsp. black pepper
- 1/4 tsp. cayenne pepper
- 1 cup milk or light cream
- bacon grease

- Veggie oil
- bacon gravy Recipe (optional, follows)

Bacon Gravy
- 1/2 lb. bacon
- 3 tbsp. bacon grease
- 3 tbsp. flour
- 1 1/2 cups light cream
- hot sauce (to taste)
- Splash brandy (optional)

DIRECTIONS

Fried Chicken

Wash and pat dry chicken

Brush with lemon juice

Sprinkle with garlic salt

Combine flour, bread crumbs, paprika, salt, pepper, and cayenne pepper - mix well

Coat chicken lightly in bread crumb mix

Dip chicken in milk/cream

Recoat in bread crumb mix

Set on rack to dry for 15 minutes

Fry bacon in large skillet, remove and reserve for Bacon Gravy (don't forget to reserve 3 tbsp. bacon grease for bacon gravy)

Add enough oil to bring bacon grease up to about 1/2-inch

Over medium heat, lightly brown chicken a few pieces at a time

When all is browned pour off half of grease

Return chicken to skillet, reduce heat, cover and cook for 20 minutes

Uncover and cook for another 10 - 15 minutes until done and crisp

Serve with bacon gravy

Bacon Gravy

Heat 3 tbsp. bacon grease

Stir in flour

Cook and stir until well blended and flour turns a light brown

Gradually stir in cream

Season with hot sauce and brandy

Bring to boil

Stir in fried, crumbled bacon

Remove from heat and serve

Bacon Fact:

Bacon contains Vitamin B12, which can help fight Anemia and boost vitality.

MASSACHUSETTS

NEW ENGLAND BACON CLAM CHOWDER

INGREDIENTS

- 4 slices bacon, diced
- 1 1/2 cups chopped onion
- 1 1/2 cups water
- 4 cups peeled and cubed potatoes
- 1 1/2 tsps. salt
- ground black pepper to taste
- 3 cups half-and-half
- 3 tbsp. butter
- 2 (10 ounce) cans minced clams

PREP 15 mins; COOK 30 mins; READY IN 45 mins

DIRECTIONS

Place diced bacon in large stock pot over medium-high heat. Cook until almost crisp; add onions, and cook 5 minutes. Stir in water and potatoes, and season with salt and pepper. Bring to a boil, and cook uncovered for 15 minutes, or until potatoes are fork tender.

Pour in half-and-half, and add butter. Drain clams, reserving clam liquid; stir clams and 1/2 of the clam liquid into the soup. Cook for about 5 minutes, or until heated through. Do not allow to boil.

MAPLE BOURBON BACON JAM

INGREDIENTS

- 1 pound thick smoked bacon, cut into 1 inch pieces
- 1 large onion, sliced
- 4 cloves garlic, chopped
- 1/4 cup cider vinegar
- 3/4 cup coffee (brewed)
- 1/4 cup brown sugar
- 1/4 cup maple syrup
- 1/4 cup bourbon
- 1-2 chipotle chilies in adobo, chopped
- 1/2 tsp. cumin
- pepper to taste

DIRECTIONS

Cook the bacon in a large sauce pan an over medium heat until the fat has rendered and the bacon starts to get crispy and set aside, reserving 1 tbsp. of the grease in the pan.

Add the onions and sauté until tender, about 5-7 minutes.

Add the garlic and sauté until fragrant, about a minute.

Add the vinegar and deglaze the pan.

Add the coffee, brown sugar, maple syrup, bourbon, bacon, chipotle chilies, cumin and pepper, reduce the heat and simmer until reduced to a syrupy consistency, about 1-2 hours.

Process the jam in a food processor to smooth it out a bit but not too much as you want to have the texture of the bacon.

If you do not finish it all in one sitting, store it in a sealed container in the fridge for up to 4 weeks.

Tip: Chipotle chili peppers in adobo can be hot and everyone has their own preferences for heat. It is recommended that you add the chipotles in adobo a bit at a time, taste testing as you go, to bring the heat up to the point where it is a nice undertone without overwhelming.

Tip: If you prefer the bacon jam warm, take out when I needed and give it a few seconds in the microwave before using it.

Bacon Fact:

The Patron Saint of Bacon is St. Anthony the Abbot; who is the patron saint of pigs, swine herders, and butchers.

MICHIGAN

MICHIGAN BACON PASTY (MEAT HAND PIE)

INGREDIENTS

- 3 cups all-purpose flour, plus extra for rolling dough
- 1 cup shortening or lard
- Kosher salt
- 1 cup ice cold water
- 8 ounces ground beef
- 10 strips of cooked bacon
- 4 ounces rutabaga, cut into 1/4-inch dice
- 1 medium carrot, cut into 1/4-inch dice
- 1 small yellow onion, finely chopped
- 1 small russet potato, peeled and cut into 1/4-inch dice
- 1/4 cup picked fresh parsley leaves, chopped
- Freshly ground black pepper
- 1 egg, whisked
- Gravy for serving

DIRECTIONS

Preheat the oven to 350 degrees F. Line a baking sheet with parchment paper.

Add the flour, shortening and a pinch of salt to a food processor and run the motor until the dough starts to clump together. With the motor running, drizzle in the water. Stop the motor when a ball begins to form. Wrap the dough in plastic and refrigerate for about 1 hour. This step allows the glutens to relax and makes for easier rolling.

Mix together the beef, bacon, rutabaga, carrots, onions, potatoes and parsley. Sprinkle with salt and pepper. Set aside until ready to form the pies.

Cut the dough into 6 even pieces, about 5 ounces each, and form into balls. Make sure the dough is cold for easier handling. Flour a work surface and roll out each ball of dough into an 8-inch circle. Evenly divide the filling (about 3/4 cup per pasty) on one half of each dough circle. Fold the dough over to cover the mixture and crimp the edges using a fork. Slice 3 small slits on top of each pocket. This prevents steam from building up and splitting the dough. Brush the pasties with the egg and bake on the prepared baking sheet until the crust is golden brown and flaky, about 1 hour 15 minutes. Serve with ketchup.

Note: Pasties can be baked and then frozen. To reheat, place in a 300 degree F oven until warmed through, about 20 minutes.

BACON & CHERRY SALSA

INGREDIENTS
- 1 1/3 cups frozen unsweetened Michigan tart cherries
- 1/2 cup of cooked bacon crumbled
- 1/4 cup coarsely chopped dried tart cherries
- 1/4 cup finely chopped red onion
- 1 tbsp. chopped fresh jalapeno pepper or to taste
- 1 clove garlic, finely chopped
- 1 tbsp. chopped fresh cilantro
- 1 tsp. cornstarch

DIRECTIONS

Coarsely chop frozen tart cherries. Let cherries thaw and drain, reserving 1 Tbs. cherry juice. When cherries are thawed, put drained cherries, dried cherries, bacon crumble, onion, jalapenos, garlic and cilantro in a medium saucepan. Mix well. In a small container, combine reserved cherry juice and cornstarch. Mix until smooth, then stir into cherry mixture. Cook, stirring constantly, over medium-high heat until mixture is thickened. Let cool.

Bacon Fact:

The price of pork bellies is the highest it has been since 1988.

MINNESOTA

MINNESOTA WILD RICE BACON CASSEROLE

INGREDIENTS

- 1 cup wild rice
- 1/2 cup of cut bacon
- 3 cups hot chicken broth
- 1/2 stick butter
- 3 tbsp. chopped onion
- 3 tbsp. chopped green pepper (or a mix of red, green and yellow peppers to add color)

DIRECTIONS

Heat butter in a frying pan over low heat. Sauté onions, bacon, and peppers. Add the wild rice and blend all together. Transfer to a casserole dish and add chicken broth.

Cover and bake at 350 degrees for 45 minutes or until all liquid is absorbed.

BACON PECAN CRUSTED MINNESOTA WALLEYE

INGREDIENTS

- 2 Minnesota walleye fillets (1/2 lb. each)
- 2 strips of bacon
- flour seasoned with salt and pepper
- 1 large egg, slightly beaten
- 3/4 cup finely chopped pecans
- 2 tbsp. butter
- 2 tbsp. minced scallion
- 3 cups all-purpose flour
- 1 ripe pear, peeled and cut into slices
- 1/4 cup white wine
- juice of 1/2 lemon
- 1/4 cup heavy cream
- 2 tbsp. blue cheese

DIRECTIONS

Dredge walleye in flour, shake off excess, dip in egg and coat in pecans and then wrap each fillet in bacon. Melt butter and sauté walleye 6 minutes on each side. Transfer fillets to a plate and cover to keep warm.

Drain excess grease. Add scallions and pear. Cook 1 to 2 minutes. Add wine and cook a few more minutes. Add cream, season with salt and pepper. Add lemon juice. At the last minute, add the blue cheese and spoon over the fish.

Bacon Fact:

A female pig is called a sow, a male is called a boar, and the baby is called a piglet.

MISSISSIPPI

MISSISSIPPI BACON MUD PIE

INGREDIENTS

- 1/4 cup of cooked bacon crumble
- 2 cups graham cracker crumbs
- 1/4 cup white sugar
- 1/2 cup butter, softened
- 1 (12 ounce) container frozen whipped topping, thawed
- 3/4 cup white sugar
- 8 ounces cream cheese, softened
- 1 (3.9 ounce) package instant chocolate pudding mix
- 1 (3.4 ounce) package instant butterscotch pudding mix
- 3 cups milk

PREP 30 mins; READY IN 30 mins

DIRECTIONS

Thoroughly blend graham cracker crumbs, 1/4 cup sugar, and butter. Press firmly in bottom of 9x13 inch pan.

Blend together half the whipped topping, 3/4 cup sugar, and softened cream cheese. Spread mixture on top of crust.

Whip together the puddings and milk and spread on top of cream cheese mixture. Top with remaining whipped topping and bacon crumble.

MISSISSIPPI MUD CHEESY POTATOES

INGREDIENTS

- 8-10 cups potatoes, diced finely
- 16 ounces cheddar cheese, cubed or shredded
- 1 cup mayonnaise (real)
- 1 package bacon, cooked and torn into large bits
- 1/2 cup green onions, chopped

DIRECTIONS

In a 9x13 pan or 3 quart casserole dish, mix potatoes, cheddar cheese, bacon, and green onions.

Stir in mayonnaise.

Bake at 325 for an hour and a half or until potatoes are tender. Top with additional cheese if desired.

Bacon Fact:
More than half of all homes keep bacon on hand at all times.

MISSOURI

FRIED BACON RAVIOLI

INGREDIENTS

- Olive oil, for frying
- 1 cup buttermilk
- 2 cups Italian-style bread crumbs
- 1 box store-bought cheese ravioli (about 24 ravioli)
- 1/4 cup freshly grated Parmesan
- 1 jar store bought marinara sauce, heated, for dipping
- 5 slices of crumbled bacon

DIRECTIONS

Pour enough olive oil into a large frying pan to reach a depth of 2 inches. Heat the oil over medium heat until a deep-fry thermometer registers 325 degrees F.

While the oil is heating, put the buttermilk and the bread crumbs in separate shallow bowls. Working in batches, dip ravioli in buttermilk to coat completely. Allow the excess buttermilk to drip back into the bowl. Dredge ravioli in the bread crumbs. Place the ravioli on a baking sheet, and continue with the remaining ravioli.

When the oil is hot, fry the ravioli in batches, turning occasionally, until golden brown, about 3 minutes. Using a slotted spoon, transfer the fried ravioli to paper towels to drain.

Sprinkle the fried ravioli with Parmesan and serve with a bowl of warmed marinara sauce for dipping. Place a desired amount of bacon crumble in marinara sauce and if desired you can sprinkle bacon crumble over whole dish.

SPINACH BACON EGG CASSEROLE

INGREDIENTS

- 8 eggs
- 3/4 cup whole milk
- 1 tsp. garlic salt
- 1/4 tsp. ground black pepper
- 1/2 pound bacon
- 1 red bell pepper, chopped
- 1/4 cup minced onion
- 1 (10 ounce) package frozen chopped spinach, thawed and drained
- 1/2 cup shredded Monterey Jack cheese
- 1/4 cup finely shredded Asiago cheese

DIRECTIONS

Preheat oven to 350 degrees F (175 degrees C). Grease a 9x13-inch baking pan.

Beat eggs in a bowl using a fork. Add milk, garlic salt, and black pepper to eggs and beat until fully integrated.

Place bacon in a large skillet and cook over medium-high heat, turning occasionally, until evenly browned, about 10 minutes. Transfer bacon to a paper towel-lined plate and drain grease from skillet. Chop bacon.

Sauté red bell pepper and onion in the same skillet over medium-high heat until tender, 5 to 10 minutes.

Spread spinach into the bottom of the prepared baking pan; top with bacon and red bell pepper mixture. Pour egg mixture over bacon mixture and sprinkle Monterey Jack cheese and Asiago cheese over egg mixture.

Bake in the preheated oven until a knife inserted in the center comes out clean, 35 to 45 minutes.

Bacon Fact:

71% of the time, bacon and eggs are eaten together at a meal.

MONTANA

BUTTERMILK CORN BREAD WITH BACON

INGREDIENTS

- 2 cups buttermilk
- 1 1/4 cups polenta (coarse cornmeal)*
- 8 ounces bacon (about 10 slices), cut into 1/2-inch pieces
- 1 cups all-purpose flour
- 1 1/2 tbsp. baking powder
- 1 tsp. salt
- 1/4 tsp. baking soda
- 1/2 cup (packed) golden brown sugar
- 3 large eggs
- 2 tbsp. honey
- 2 tbsp. (1/4 stick) butter, melted
- 2 1/2 cups frozen corn kernels, thawed (about 13 ounces)

  *Available at Italian markets, natural foods stores and some supermarkets.

DIRECTIONS

Stir buttermilk and polenta in medium bowl to blend. Cover and let stand at room temperature overnight. Preheat oven to 350°F. Cook bacon in heavy large skillet until crisp. Using slotted spoon, transfer bacon to paper towels to drain. Spoon 2 tablespoons bacon drippings into 13x9x2-inch metal baking pan. Tilt pan to coat bottom and sides of pan with bacon drippings. Place baking pan in oven until bacon drippings are hot, about 6 minutes.

Meanwhile, sift flour, baking powder, salt and baking soda into large bowl. Stir in brown sugar. Whisk eggs, honey and melted butter in another large bowl to blend. Stir in polenta mixture. Add to dry ingredients. Stir just until blended. Stir in corn kernels. Transfer batter to prepared hot baking pan. Sprinkle bacon over batter, then press bacon gently to submerge slightly. Bake corn bread until tester inserted into center comes out clean and top is golden, about 45 minutes. Transfer to rack. Cool 15 minutes. (Can be prepared 8 hours ahead. Cool completely. Cover and let stand at room temperature.) Cut corn bread into squares and serve warm or at room temperature.

BEEF STEW WITH BACON

INGREDIENTS

- 4 oz. thick-cut bacon, chopped
- 3 tbsp. flour
- 1 tsp. salt, plus more, to taste
- 1/2 tsp. freshly ground pepper, plus more, to taste
- 3 lb. boneless beef chuck, trimmed of excess fat and cut into chunks
- 3/4 lb. fresh cremini mushrooms, halved if large
- 1/2 lb. baby carrots
- 1/2 lb. frozen pearl onions
- 3 garlic cloves, minced
- 1 cup dry red wine
- 1 cup beef broth
- 2 tbsp. tomato paste

- 1 tbsp. minced fresh rosemary

DIRECTIONS

Cook the bacon

In a large fry pan over medium heat, cook the bacon, stirring occasionally, until crisp, 5 to 7 minutes. Transfer the bacon to paper towels to drain. Pour off the drippings into a small heatproof bowl, leaving about 1 Tbs. drippings in the pan. Set the pan, reserved drippings and bacon aside.

Brown the beef

In a sealable plastic bag, combine the flour, the 1 tsp. salt and the 1/2 tsp. pepper. Add the beef chunks and shake to coat evenly with the flour mixture. Return the fry pan to medium-high heat. When the drippings are hot, add half of the beef chunks and cook, turning once, until well browned, about 5 minutes on each side. Transfer the beef to the slow cooker. Repeat with the remaining beef chunks, adding the reserved drippings if needed. Scatter the mushrooms, carrots, onions and garlic on top.

Cook the stew

Return the pan to medium-high heat and add the wine, broth and tomato paste. Mix well, bring to a boil and deglaze the pan, stirring to scrape up the browned bits on the pan bottom. Pour the contents of the pan over the vegetables and beef. Cover and cook on the high-heat setting for 4 to 5 hours or the low-heat setting for 8 to 9 hours. The beef should be very tender. Stir in the reserved bacon and the rosemary. Cook, uncovered, on the high-heat setting for 10 minutes more to thicken the sauce slightly. Season with salt and pepper and serve. Serves 6.

Bacon Fact:
Thick sliced bacon is 1/8 inch thick. (10-14 slices/lb.)

NEBRASKA

NEBRASKA HANDHELD BACON MEAT PIES

INGREDIENTS

DOUGH:

- 1/2 cup warm water (110 to 115 degrees F)
- 1 packet active dry yeast
- 1/4 cup sugar
- 3/4 cup milk
- 6 tbsp. unsalted butter
- 4 1/4 cups all-purpose flour
- 1 1/2 tsps. kosher salt

FILLING:

- 3 tbsp. vegetable oil
- 1 pound ground beef
- 2 cups of cut cooked bacon
- 2 1/2 tsps. kosher salt, plus more if needed
- 3 cups chopped green cabbage (about 1/2 large head)
- 2 cups chopped onion (about 1 large onion)
- 1 tsp. ground white pepper
- 2 tbsp. unsalted butter, melted, for brushing
- Ketchup, for serving

DIRECTIONS

For the dough: Whisk together the warm water, yeast and 1 tsp. of the sugar in a bowl. Set aside until the yeast activates and becomes foamy on top, about 10 minutes.

Heat the milk and butter in a small pot until the butter melts. Allow to cool to less than 115 degrees F.

Whisk the flour, salt and remaining sugar in the bowl of a stand mixer fitted with a dough hook. Add the foamy yeast mixture and cooled milk and butter. Turn on the mixer to knead the dough for about 5 minutes. The dough should be a smooth uniform ball that no longer sticks to the sides of the bowl. Cover the bowl with plastic wrap and put in a warm area until the dough doubles in size, about 1 1/2 hours.

For the filling: In the meantime, heat 1 tbsp. vegetable oil over high heat in a large skillet. Add the ground beef and bacon and sprinkle with 1 1/2 tsps. salt. Brown the beef and bacon mixture, breaking it up into small pieces, about 5 minutes. Once browned, transfer the beef to a bowl and add the remaining 2 tbsp. of oil to the skillet. Reduce the heat to medium, add the cabbage and onions, season with the remaining 1 tsp salt and cook until soft, about 15 minutes. Add the browned beef back to the skillet and continue cooking an additional 5 minutes with the cabbage and onions. Season with the white pepper and additional salt if needed. Take off the heat and set aside to cool completely.

Preheat the oven to 350 degrees F. When the dough has doubled in size, punch it down and divide it into 10 equal-size balls, about 3 1/2 ounces each. Roll out each ball one at a time into a rectangle, roughly 6 by 8 inches. Spread 1/2 cup cooled filling in the center of the rectangle. Bring the two long sides of dough together so the seam is facing up and pinch them together. Pinch the short ends shut as well. You should have a rectangular shape. Put the filled dough seam-side down on a parchment-lined baking sheet. Repeat with the remaining 9 balls. You will need 2 baking sheets to fit all 10 meat pies. Cover the meat pies with a dish towel and allow them to rest for about 20 minutes. Bake in the oven until golden brown, 20 to 25 minutes.

Melt the butter. As soon as the meat pies come out of the oven, brush the tops with the melted butter. Serve with ketchup.

Note: After they have baked and cooled you can freeze up to a month. To reheat, take right out of the freezer, cover with foil and place into a 350 degree oven until heated through, 20 to 25 minutes.

QUICK BACON-CHEDDAR BISCUITS

INGREDIENTS
- 2 cups flour
- 1 tbsp. baking powder
- Kosher salt
- 1 tsp. paprika
- 1 tsp. onion powder
- 1 cup milk
- 1/2 cup butter, melted
- 8 strips bacon, cooked until crispy and crumbled
- 1 cup shredded Cheddar cheese
- 1 egg

DIRECTIONS
Heat the oven to 425 degrees F.

In a large bowl add the flour, baking powder, 1 teaspoon of salt, paprika, and onion powder. Mix to blend then make a well in the center of the bowl and add the milk, butter, bacon and cheese. Mix gently with a wooden spoon. The dough will be wet and sticky. Using a 1/4 cup measure or ice cream scoop, portion the batter onto a baking sheet, leaving an inch or so around each biscuit.

In a small bowl, beat the egg with a splash of water and then brush this mixture on the top of each biscuit. Bake in the oven until the biscuits are golden brown and a toothpick inserted in the center of one comes out clean, 20 to 22 minutes.

Bacon Fact:

John Fargginary, a Parisian butcher created a formula for Bacon Cologne in 1920.

NEVADA

VENISON GARLIC BACON HAMBURGER

Makes 6 Hamburgers

INGREDIENTS
- 1 lb. ground venison burger (bacon and garlic recipe here)
- 2 tbsp. barbeque sauce (use your favorite)
- 1/2 cup breadcrumbs
- 1 egg
- A pinch of salt and pepper
- 2 tbsp. butter
- 12 slices sharp cheddar cheese
- 6 slices thick dry cured or peppered bacon
- 6 Hamburger buns

DIRECTIONS

In a bowl, mix together bacon and garlic venison burger with salt, pepper, barbeque sauce, a whole egg and breadcrumbs. Shape into 6 hamburger patties. Let the meat rest for 15 minutes.

Cook bacon in a cast iron skillet until fully cooked. Remove and set aside on a paper towel. Remove 95% of the bacon fat from skillet.

Set your oven to broil.

Heat cast iron skillet over medium-high heat, melt 2 tbsp. butter with bacon fat. Place burgers in skillet and cook for approximately 6-7 minutes or until browned. Turn and continue to cook on the other side.

Remove from heat. Cut bacon in half and top each hamburger with 2 thick slices and 2 slices of cheddar cheese. Place cast iron skillet under the broiler until the cheese has melted. Remove from oven.

Place the venison hamburger on your favorite hamburger bun, add a slice of crisp white onion and pour your favorite barbeque sauce all over the top. Squeeze together and enjoy!

BACON-WRAPPED DATES

INGREDIENTS

- 16-ounce package of bacon (regular thickness, not thick cut), cut into thirds
- 8-ounce package of pitted dates

DIRECTIONS

Preheat the oven to 350°F. Position oven rack in the center of the oven. Cover a cookie sheet with tin foil.

Wrap a piece of bacon around a date. Make sure the bacon seam is placed facing downward on the cookie sheet. Press firmly on the bacon-wrapped date, so it is less likely to unravel. Repeat until all of the dates are wrapped in bacon.

Bake for 20-25 minutes until crisp. Let cool for 10-15 minutes before serving.

Bacon Fact:

The average person eats bacon at breakfast 12 times a year.

NEW HAMPSHIRE

CRUNCHY BACON CHEDDAR MAC & CHEESE

INGREDIENTS

- 1 lb. Casserole Macaroni
- 1 package of cooked Bacon
- 1 pint Sour cream
- 8oz package of cream cheese
- 8oz shredded Monterey Jack cheese
- 16oz Cabot Farmhouse Reserve –shredded
- ¼ tsp. Cayenne Pepper
- ¼ tsp. Paprika
- 2 cups of Milk

DIRECTIONS

1. Using a frying pan, spread a thin layer of shredded cheddar and your choice of bacon measure and cook until browned and crispy, but not burned (you may need to flip it). Repeat until you have crisped 8 oz. of the cheddar. Set this aside and crush into a crumble once cooled.

2. Soften the cream cheese and mix all ingredients including rest of bacon and melt on lowest heat stirring constantly.

3. Once the sauce is melted and creamy add the pasta.

4. Cook pasta in salted water (do not rinse) till Al-denti

5. Stir in Crispy Cheddar crumble prior to serving.

POTATO, BACON, and GRUYÈRE SOUP

INGREDIENTS

- 4 slices bacon, chopped
- 3 medium onions, chopped fine
- 3 cups chicken broth
- 3 1/4 cups water
- 3 pounds boiling potatoes (preferably yellow-fleshed)
- 1/4 cup all-purpose flour
- 1/2 pound Gruyère cheese, grated (about 2 1/2 cups)
- 1 tbsp. Madeira or Sherry if desired
- 1 tsp. Worcestershire sauce
- 3 tbsp. minced fresh parsley leaves

DIRECTIONS

In a heavy kettle (at least 5 quarts) cook bacon over moderate heat, stirring, until crisp and spoon off all but 1 tbsp. fat. Add onions and sauté over moderately high heat, stirring, until pale golden. Add broth and 3 cups of water and bring to a boil.

Peel potatoes and cut into 3/4-inch cubes. Add potatoes to soup and simmer, covered, 10 minutes.

In a small bowl whisk together flour and remaining 1/4 cup water until smooth and add to simmering soup, whisking. Simmer soup, covered, 5 minutes.

In a blender purée Gruyère with 3 cups hot soup broth. Stir purée into soup with Madeira, Worcestershire sauce, and salt and pepper to taste and remove soup from heat. Soup may be prepared up to this point 3 days ahead (cool uncovered before chilling covered). Reheat over low heat but do not let boil.

Just before serving, stir in parsley.

Bacon Fact:
19% of all pork eaten in the home is in bacon form.

NEW JERSEY

BEAR BACON MEATLOAF

INGREDIENTS

- 3 lbs. ground bear meat
- 1 package of Bacon
- 1 lb. ground beef (high % fat)
- 3 cans Campbell's French onion soup
- 3 eggs
- 1 1/2 cups bread crumbs
- 1 can mushrooms 8 oz. or larger
- 1/4 cup ketchup
- garlic powder (to taste)
- black pepper (to taste)

DIRECTIONS

Drain the broth out of 2 cans of the French onion soup and set aside. Combine meat and all other ingredients (except 3rd can of soup) into a mixing bowl. Add the onions from the 2 cans of soup you drained earlier and mix well. Put into roasting pan and pour broth. Make a bacon lattice, place bacon over meatloaf and the 3rd can of onion soup over top. Bake at 350 degrees for 2 ½ hours or until done.

THREE CHEESE GRILLED CHEESE and BACON SANDWICH

INGREDIENTS

- 2 slices Pain au levain or soft-textured white or sourdough bread
- 1 tbsp. of butter or lemon butter (butter blended with a bit of
- lemon zest and grated fresh garlic)
- 1 tbsp. ricotta cheese
- 1/4 cup grated parmesan cheese
- 3 slices crisp-cooked bacon, crumbled
- 1-2 slices provolone cheese

DIRECTIONS

1. Heat oven to 350 degrees (optional). Spread butter on the outer side of both bread slices.

2. Assemble grilled cheese: spread unbuttered side of one bread slice with ricotta then add grated Parmesan and bacon. Top with Provolone and second slice of bread, buttered side up.

3. Heat a medium oven-safe, non-stick pan over medium heat for about 3 minutes until hot. Place sandwich into pan, toast until golden brown. Flip and grill until second side is golden brown, or transfer oven-safe pan to the warmed oven for 5-7 minutes until cheeses are melted and oozy and both sides are well browned.

Bacon Fact:
Males prefer bacon slightly more than females do.

NEW MEXICO

BACON and GREEN CHILI QUICHE

INGREDIENTS

- 1 refrigerated pie crust (half of 15-ounce package), room temperature
- 8 strips bacon
- 1 4-ounce can diced green chilies, drained
- 4 green onions, chopped
- 1 cup shredded Monterey Jack cheese (about 4 ounces)
- 1 cup shredded sharp cheddar cheese (about 4 ounces)
- 1 1/4 cups half and half
- 4 eggs
- 1/2 tsp. salt

DIRECTIONS

Preheat oven to 425°F. Unfold crust. Using wet fingertips press together any tears. Press crust into 9-inch deep dish pie plate. Press foil over crust to hold shape. Bake 5 minutes. Remove from oven; remove foil. Reduce temperature to 400°F.

Cook bacon in heavy large skillet over medium-high heat until brown and crisp. Transfer to paper towels and drain. Crumble bacon. Sprinkle bacon, then chilies and green onion over crust. Combine Monterey Jack cheese and cheddar cheese and sprinkle over. Beat half and half, eggs and salt in medium bowl to blend. Pour half and half mixture into crust.

Bake quiche until knife inserted into center comes out clean, about 45 minutes. Let quiche stand 5 minutes. Cut quiche into wedges and serve.

BACON WRAPPED STUFFED CHILES

INGREDIENTS

- 12 large Green Chile Peppers (Or if you can't find Green Chiles any grocery store Pepper/Chile will work)
- 4 medium Boneless/Skinless Chicken Breasts (or one whole cooked rotisserie Chicken form the store)
- 1 lb. Bacon
- 1 container of Cream Cheese
- 2 cups or so, of Shredded Pepper Jack Cheese
- 3 tbsp. Chile powder
- 3 tbsp. Oregano
- A drizzle of Olive Oil
- Salt and pepper to taste

DIRECTIONS

Heat a large pot of water to boiling. Add the Chile Peppers and boil them for 4 minutes, remove them from the pot and let them drain & cool on some paper towel.

Preheat the oven to 400 degrees. Place the Chicken on a baking sheet. Drizzle it with some Olive Oil and salt and pepper to taste. Roast the chicken until it's fully cooked and tender. This step can be skipped if you use a store bought Roasted Whole Chicken; a terrific time saver!

Let the chicken cool and then shred it using two forks.

Take each cooled Chile pepper and carefully make a slit from the top of the pepper almost to the bottom point. Remove seeds (rinsing them under cold water works great)

Add the Chile Powder & Oregano into a pie plate or shallow dish mix well to combine and set aside.

In a large bowl add the Shredded Chicken, Cream Cheese and Pepper Jack Cheese combine well!

Take each prepared Chile and stuff it with 2-3 tbsp. of the Chicken/cheese mixture, depending on the size of the pepper.

Wrap the pepper with the Bacon, and roll it in the Chile Powder/Oregano mixture.

Place the pepper stuffing side up, onto the prepared baking rack. Making sure to tuck the bacon ends under the Chile to bake.

Bake for 25-30 minutes at 375 degrees or until the Bacon is crispy and the Pepper is tender!

Serve these while they're warm, crispy & melty!

Bacon Fact:

Women who are pregnant should eat bacon. Bacon contains Choline, which helps in fetal brain development.

NEW YORK

DANGER DOGS (BACON WRAPPED HOT DOGS)

INGREDIENTS

- 8 hot dogs
- 8 hot dog buns
- 8 strips of bacon
- 1 large onion (sliced)
- 3-4 jalapenos (seeded and sliced)
- 2 tbsp. Oil
- (optional) relish, ketchup, mustard

DIRECTIONS

Cut the onion into slices.

Cut the jalapenos in half, remove the seeds, and then slice them lengthwise into 1/8 inch wide strips.

Wrap a strip of bacon tightly around each hot dog.

Heat oil over medium high heat in a large pan. Add the onions and peppers, but keep the onions and peppers separate from each other. cook them until soft and a little brown (about 12 minutes).

Meanwhile, cook the bacon-wrapped hot dogs in another pan over medium heat. Turn the hot dogs occasionally until the bacon is crisp on all sides (about 12 minutes)

After the hot dogs are cooked, just stick them in a bun and top them with the sautéed onions and peppers to taste. You can add ketchup or mustard, but the traditional condiment is mayo.

BACON and SMOKED GOUDA PIZZA

INGREDIENTS

- 1 New York style pizza dough
- 3 Roma tomatoes, sliced and oven roasted
- 1 Vidalia Onion, caramelized
- 3-4 slices of butcher cut bacon, cooked and diced
- 50g Smoked Gouda (1.5 ounces)
- 90g Fresh Mozzarella (3 ounces)

Tools Used Medium Mixing Bowl Digital Food Scale Pizza Stone Wood Pizza Peel Turner / Flat Spatula Cast Iron Skillet or heavy bottom pan Chef's Knife Half Sheet Baking Pan Parchment Paper or Silpat Large Cutting Board

DIRECTIONS

Make and proof dough as per instructions. Preheat oven to 400°F (205°C). Slice and caramelize onions as per instructions. Slice and roast tomatoes. Cook bacon as per instructions. Preheat oven and baking stone to 550°F (288°C) for 45 minutes. Form dough on lightly floured wooden pizza peel to 12-13" circle. Add slices of roasted tomatoes to dough. Add caramelized onions as evenly as possible to dough. Add smoked gouda and fresh mozzarella evenly. Lastly add bacon. Bake on baking stone for approximately 5 minutes until golden crust and bottom. Use pizza peel to remove pizza from oven. Allow to cool for two minutes before cutting.

Bacon Fact:
The Italian bacon specialty made of pork cheeks is called 'Guanciale."

NORTH CAROLINA

BACON DIP

INGREDIENTS

- 10 slices bacon, crisp-cooked, drained and crumbled
- 1 - 8 ounce package softened cream cheese (or whipped)
- 1 tsp. vinegar
- 2 tbsp. cream
- 3 Green onions, chopped
- 1 tsp. horseradish (may add more to taste)
- 2 tbsp. green olives, chopped

DIRECTIONS

Mix cream cheese and vinegar until smooth. Add onion, horseradish, bacon and olives. Blend well.

BACON-WRAPPED PORK with SPICY MANGO-BASIL RELISH

Tropical and light, grill these bacon-wrapped chops for a summer meal. Serve with grilled seasonal vegetables and steamed rice.

Servings: 4

INGREDIENTS

- 4 boneless pork chops,1 1/2-inch thick

- 8 strips bacon
- 1/2 cup soy sauce
- 1/2 cup fresh lime juice
- 1 1/2 tsps. cayenne pepper
- 2 to 3 cloves fresh garlic, minced
- Spicy Mango-Basil Relish (recipe follows)

DIRECTIONS

Wrap 2 strips of bacon around the outside edge of each pork chop, securing in several places with toothpicks. Mix together the soy sauce, lime juice, cayenne pepper and garlic. Reserve half of the mixture for basting and place half in a shallow baking dish. Add pork to dish and turn to coat both sides. Cover and refrigerate for at least 1 hour, turning pork occasionally. (Marinate longer for more flavor.) Remove from marinade, discard marinade, and place pork on grill over medium coals. Cook for 12 to 16 minutes total, basting with reserved marinade several times, until pork is 160°F., as measured with an instant-read thermometer. Serve with a large dollop of Spicy Mango-Basil Relish.

Spicy Mango-Basil Relish: In a small bowl stir together 1 peeled, pitted and chopped mango, 2 tbsp. fresh lime juice, and 2 tbsps. chopped fresh basil and 1/4 tsp cayenne pepper.

Bacon Fact:
59% of bacon is consumed on weekdays.

NORTH DAKOTA

NORTH DAKOTA BAKED BEANS

INGREDIENTS

- 1 lb. hamburger
- 1 lb. bacon, chopped
- 1 onion
- 2 cans lima beans
- 2 cans pork and beans
- 2 cans kidney beans
- 1 cup brown sugar
- 1 cup ketchup
- 1 tsp. - 1 tbsp. prepared mustard, to taste
- 1 tbsp. vinegar

DIRECTIONS

Brown hamburger, onion and bacon; drain off fat. Add remaining ingredients. Mix and bake 45 minutes at 350 degrees. Good served with corn bread.

POTATO BACON CASSEROLE

Tender hash browns and succulent bacon pieces are at the heart of this hearty potato dish. A crowd-pleaser at brunch or any meal.

Preparation Time - 10 minutes

Cooking Time - 60 minutes

INGREDIENTS

- 4 cups frozen shredded hash brown potatoes
- 1/2 cup finely chopped onion
- 8 ounces bacon or turkey bacon, cooked and crumbled
- 1 cup (4 oz.) shredded cheddar cheese
- 1 can (12 fl. oz.) Evaporated Milk
- 1 large egg, lightly beaten or 1/4 cup egg substitute
- 1 1/2 tsps. seasoned salt

DIRECTIONS

PREHEAT oven to 350 F. Grease 8-inch-square baking dish.

LAYER 1/2 potatoes, 1/2 onion, 1/2 bacon and 1/2 cheese in prepared baking dish; repeat layers. Combine evaporated milk, egg and seasoned salt in small bowl. Pour evenly over potato mixture; cover.

BAKE for 55 to 60 minutes. Uncover; bake for an additional 5 minutes. Let stand for 10 to 15 minutes before serving.

Yields 6 servings

OHIO

BACON BUCKEYES

INGREDIENTS

- 6-20oz Jar Peanut Butter
- Sticks Butter
- 2 lbs. Powdered Sugar
- Chocolate for Dipping
- Bacon
- Kosher Salt (optional)

DIRECTIONS

Mix peanut butter, butter & powdered sugar slightly. Place in Oven at 200 degrees to soften. Mix well and add cooked, chopped bacon. Taste, add more sugar if desired. Form into small balls (1 inch) and refrigerate until cooled. Melt chocolate or chocolate chips in double boiler or in microwave. To microwave, heat for 30 seconds, stir, then repeat in 10-15 second increments. Use toothpick to dip balls into chocolate, leaving some peanut butter showing. Top with a few bacon pieces and (optional) sprinkle with kosher salt, chipotle pepper or a spice of your choice. Cool on wax paper.

ADDITIONAL IDEAS

Sprinkle Sweet & Savory Buckeyes with a little bit of kosher salt, chipotle pepper, tajin or other delicious spices to give it an extra kick!

For Peanut Butter & Jelly Buckeyes, add fresh strawberries, dip, and chill and serve quickly

To achieve better chocolate for dipping and setting, use chocolate confectionary coating or add shortening or paraffin wax to the chocolate

CHEESY BACON BOMBS

INGREDIENTS

- 1 can (8ct.) Pillsbury Grands Flaky Layers Biscuits
- Cubed Mozzarella Cheese (1-1″ cube per Bomb)
- 2 lbs. of Bacon (1 slice per Bomb)
- Sticks
- Oil for frying (I used Canola)

DIRECTIONS

Cube up the Cheese, and cut each Biscuit into fourths. Place one piece of Cheese inside a Biscuit quarter, and roll, nice and tight. Wrap each rolled Bomb in a slice of bacon, and secure it with a skewer or toothpick. In a med/large pot, heat up approx. 2″ of oil (to 350 degrees) and fry them up in small batches. Maybe one or two at a time, the oil will expand so stay close.

Drain them on some Paper Towel, but serve them up good and warm, so they do this. Take a good, close look at them before you share them, because they'll be gone in a matter of seconds

Bacon Fact:

"Bacoun" once referred to all pork. During the 17th century, "Bacon" referred only to cured pork.

OKLAHOMA

RUSTIC BACON-APPLE PIE

INGREDIENTS

- Rustic Bacon-Apple Pie
- 2 tsps. cornstarch
- 1 tsp. vanilla extract
- 1/4 cup plus 1 tbsp. water
- 1 tbsp. unsalted butter
- 1 tsp. canola oil
- 6 apples, a mix of tart and sweet, such as Granny Smith and Golden Delicious, cut into quarters, cored, and thinly sliced crosswise
- 1/3 cup packed light or dark brown sugar
- 1 tsp. fresh lemon juice
- 1/2 tsp. kosher salt
- All-purpose flour, for rolling

Cheddar Bacon Crust:

- 1 large egg, beaten 2 tbsp. coarse sugar
- 1/2 tsp. kosher salt
- 1/3 cup cold water
- 2 ounces thick-cut bacon, finely diced and frozen
- 2 cups all-purpose flour
- 2 ounces sharp cheddar cheese, grated (1/2 cup) and chilled
- 8 tbsp. (1 stick) unsalted butter, cut into 1/4-inch-thick slices and chilled

DIRECTIONS

Cheddar Bacon Crust: In a small bowl, stir the salt into the cold water until it dissolves. In the bowl of a food processor, use your hands to toss the bacon with the flour until well coated. Pulse until coarse crumbs form. Transfer to a large bowl. Toss the cheese and butter into the flour mixture, and then press in the butter with your fingertips until coarse crumbs form with a few bigger pieces remaining. Add the salted water all at once, and quickly gather the dough with your hands into a large, shaggy clump.

Divide the dough into 2 equal pieces, shape into disks, cover tightly with plastic wrap, and chill until firm, at least 1 hour and up to 3 days.

Rustic Bacon-Apple Tart: In a small bowl, stir together the cornstarch, vanilla, and 1/4 cup water until smooth.

In a very large skillet, melt the butter in the oil over medium-high heat. Add the apples and cook, tossing and stirring occasionally, until lightly charred, about 5 minutes.

Add the brown sugar, lemon juice, and salt. Cook, stirring frequently, until the sugar dissolves, about 2 minutes. Add the cornstarch mixture and cook, stirring, until the liquid thickens, about 1 minute. Remove from the heat and let cool completely.

Preheat the oven to 375F. Line a large rimmed baking sheet with parchment paper.

On a lightly floured surface and using a lightly floured rolling pin, roll each piece of dough into a 1/ 4 -inch-thick round. Transfer to the prepared baking sheet. Divide the cooled filling between the two rounds, leaving a 2-inch border. Fold and pleat the border up and around the apples, leaving the center open.

In a small bowl, beat the remaining 1 table- spoon water into the egg. Brush the egg wash over the dough, and sprinkle with the coarse sugar. Bake until the crust is golden brown, about 45 minutes. Cool completely on a wire rack.

CRISPY BACON-WRAPPED CORNMEAL OKRA

INGREDIENTS

- 4 cups vegetable oil
- 1/4 cup all-purpose flour
- 1/2 cup cornmeal
- 1/2 tsp. freshly ground black pepper
- 1/2 tsp. ground paprika
- 1/2 tsp. garlic powder
- 2 egg whites
- Kosher salt
- 2 cups fresh okra, washed and dried well, tips removed

Chipotle Sour Cream:
- 1 cup sour cream
- Juice of 1/2 lime
- 1 canned chipotle pepper in adobo sauce, finely chopped
- Kosher salt and freshly ground black pepper
- 1 to 2 packages of Bacon (depending on the amount of okra)

DIRECTIONS

In a large, heavy-bottomed pan, heat the vegetable oil over medium heat until a deep-frying thermometer inserted in the oil reaches 350 degrees F.

Prepare a baking tray lined with paper towels.

Combine the flour, cornmeal, black pepper, paprika, and garlic powder in a shallow bowl.

Put the egg whites and a pinch of salt into another bowl, and whisk until the mixture is frothy. Dip the okra in the egg whites and allow the excess egg whites to drip off, then dip the okra into the flour mixture, shake off the excess flour, wrap with a strip of bacon, and gently drop into the preheated oil.

Fry the vegetables until golden brown, turning frequently for even color.

Transfer the fried okra to a tray, lined with paper towels to absorb the excess oil, and season with salt, to taste. Coat, and fry, and season the remaining okra. Serve with the Chipotle Sour Cream.

Combine the sour cream, lime juice, chopped chipotle pepper, and salt, and pepper to taste, in a bowl. Mix to incorporate well. Serve the dipping sauce alongside the Crispy Cornmeal Okra.

Bacon Fact:

A single serving of bacon is 3 medium-thickness slices.

OREGON

OREGON PEPPERED BACON AND CRAB BLT

INGREDIENTS

- 1 red bell pepper (capsicum)
- 1/2 cup mayonnaise
- 1 tbsp. chopped fresh tarragon
- 6 ounces thick-sliced pepper bacon
- 4 crusty artisan bread rolls, split and lightly toasted
- 1 1/2 cups fresh-cooked dungeness crabmeat, picked over for shell fragments
- 2 ripe tomatoes, sliced 1/4 inch thick
- 1 small head Boston lettuce or 1 small bibb lettuce, leaves separated

DIRECTIONS

Preheat the broiler (griller).

Cut the bell pepper in half lengthwise and remove the stern, seeds, and ribs.

Place, cut sides down, on a baking sheet.

Broil (grill) until the skin blackens and blisters.

Remove from the broiler, drape loosely with aluminum foil, and let cool for 10 minutes, then peel away the skin.

Chop finely and place in a small bowl.

Add the mayonnaise and tarragon and mix well.

Meanwhile, in a large frying pan over medium-high heat, fry the bacon until crisp, about 10 minutes.

Using tongs, transfer to paper towels to drain.

Spread the cut surfaces of the rolls with the mayonnaise mixture, dividing it evenly between the tops and bottoms.

Place the bottoms of the rolls on individual plates and top with the crabmeat, tomatoes, bacon, and lettuce.

Cover with the roll tops and secure each sandwich with 2 toothpicks.

Cut each sandwich in half between the toothpicks and serve.

BACON WRAPPED CITRUS SCALLOPS

INGREDIENTS

- 12 slices bacon
- 24 large sea scallops
- 3/4 cup maple syrup
- 2 tbsp. butter
- 3 tbsp. orange juice (fresh is best)
- 1 tsp. grated orange peel

DIRECTIONS

Cut each bacon slice in half. Cook over medium heat 5-6 minutes.

Wrap each scallop in a bacon piece.

In a saucepan over medium-high heat, bring syrup to a boil. Cook, uncovered, about 5 minutes, until reduced to about 2/3 cup.

Remove from heat. Add butter, orange juice, and orange peel and stir until butter is melted and mixture is combined.

Coat grill rack with cooking spray. Heat grill to a medium-high heat (350-400 degrees).

Using 6 skewers, thread 4 wrapped scallops onto each skewer (if using wooden, soak in water for about 30 minutes first). Brush syrup mixture over scallops.

Grill scallops for 4-6 minutes, turning once or twice, until scallops are opaque and bacon is crisp.

Bacon Fact:
Oscar Mayer patented the first packed, sliced bacon in 1924.

PENNSYLVANIA

PHILLY BACON CHEESE STEAK

INGREDIENTS

- 2 to 2 1/2 pound strip loin, trimmed
- Olive oil
- Salt and freshly ground black pepper
- Soft hoagie rolls, split 3/4 open
- 12 strips of bacon
- Provolone Sauce
- Sautéed Mushrooms
- Caramelized Onions
- Sautéed Peppers

PROVOLONE SAUCE

- 1 tbsp. unsalted butter
- 1 tbsp. all-purpose flour
- 2 cups whole milk, heated
- 1 cup grated aged provolone cheese
- 1/4 cup grated Parmigiano-Reggiano
- 1 tsp. kosher salt
- 1/4 tsp. freshly ground black pepper

SAUTEED PEPPERS

- 2 tbsp. olive oil
- 2 poblano peppers, thinly sliced
- 2 Cubano peppers, thinly sliced

- Salt and freshly ground black pepper

CARAMELIZED ONIONS
- 2 tbsps. unsalted butter
- 1 tbsp. canola oil
- 3 large Spanish onions, peeled, halved and thinly sliced
- 1 tsp. kosher salt
- 1/4 tsp. freshly ground black pepper

SAUTEED MUSHROOMS
- 2 tbsps. olive oil
- 1 tbsp. unsalted butter
- 1 1/2 pounds mushrooms (cremini and shiitake), coarsely chopped
- 3 tbsps. finely chopped fresh parsley leaves
- Salt and freshly ground black pepper

DIRECTIONS
Place steak in freezer for 30 to 45 minutes; this makes it easier to slice the meat. Remove the meat from the freezer and slice very thinly.

Heat griddle or grill pan over high heat. Brush steak slices with oil and season with salt and pepper. Cook for 45 to 60 seconds per side.

Place several slices of the meat on the bottom half of the roll, place bacon strips as needed, spoon some of the cheese sauce over the meat, and top with the mushrooms, onions, and peppers.

Melt butter in a medium saucepan over medium heat. Whisk in the flour and cook for 1 minute. Slowly whisk in the warm milk, and cook, whisking constantly until thickened, about 4 to 5 minutes. Remove the mixture from the heat and whisk in the provolone and Parmesan until combined; season with the salt and pepper.

Heat butter and oil in a large sauté pan over medium heat. Add the onions, season with salt and pepper, and cook slowly until golden brown and caramelized, stirring occasionally, approximately 30 to 40 minutes.

Heat oil and butter in a large sauté pan over high heat. Add the mushrooms and cook until the mushrooms are golden brown. Stir in the parsley and season with salt and pepper.

Heat the oil in medium sauté pan over high heat. Add the peppers and cook until soft. Season with salt and pepper.

PENNSYLVANIA DUTCH HOT BACON DRESSING

INGREDIENTS

- 3 slices bacon, crisp and chopped
- 1 egg, well beaten
- 1 1/2 tbsp. flour
- 1 cup milk
- 1/4 cup vinegar
- 1/4 cup sugar
- 1/2 tsp. salt
- salad greens (lettuce, endive, spinach or dandelion)
- chopped onion (optional)

DIRECTIONS

Cook bacon until crisp; remove and chop.

Add to greens.

Add all other ingredients to the beaten egg and pour into the hot bacon fat and cook until thickened.

Serve over greens, and add a little bit of chopped onion to salad, if desired.

Bacon Fact:

Denmark consumes the most bacon in the world.

RHODE ISLAND

RHODE ISLAND CLAM CHOWDER

INGREDIENTS

- 24 medium-size quahog clams, usually rated "top neck" or "cherrystone," rinsed
- 1 tbsp. unsalted butter
- ¼ pound slab bacon or salt pork, diced
- 1 large Spanish onion, diced
- 2 large ribs celery, cleaned and diced
- 12 red bliss potatoes, cubed
- ½ cup dry white wine
- 3 sprigs thyme
- 1 bay leaf
- Freshly ground black pepper to taste
- ¼ cup chopped parsley.

DIRECTIONS

Put the clams in a large, heavy Dutch oven, add about 4 cups water, and then set over medium-high heat. Cover, and cook until clams have opened, approximately 10 to 15 minutes. (Clams that fail to open after 15 to 20 minutes should be discarded.) Strain clam broth through a sieve lined with cheesecloth or doubled-up paper towels, and set aside. Remove clams from shells, and set those aside as well.

Rinse out the pot, and return it to the stove. Add butter, and turn heat to medium-low. Add the bacon or salt pork, and cook, stirring occasionally, until the fat has rendered and the pork has started to brown, approximately 5 to 7 minutes. Use a slotted spoon to remove pork from fat, and set aside.

Add onions and celery to the fat, and cook, stirring frequently, until they are soft but not brown, about 10 minutes. Stir in potatoes and wine, and continue cooking until the wine has evaporated and the potatoes have just started to soften, approximately 5 minutes. Add 4 cups of clam broth, reserving the rest for another use. Add the thyme and the bay leaf.

Partly cover the pot, and simmer gently until potatoes are tender, approximately 10 to 15 minutes.

Meanwhile, chop the clams into bits that are about the size of the bacon dice.

When the potatoes are tender, stir in the chopped clams and reserved bacon. Add black pepper to taste. Let the chowder come just to a simmer, and remove from heat. Fish out the thyme and bay leaf, and discard.

The chowder should be allowed to sit for a while to cure. Reheat it before serving, then garnish with chopped parsley. Serve with oyster crackers.

JOHNNYCAKE

INGREDIENTS
- 1 cup white cornmeal
- 3/4 tsp. salt
- 1 cup water
- 1/2 cup milk
- Bacon drippings

DIRECTIONS

In a medium bowl, place cornmeal and salt.

In a medium saucepan over high heat, bring water to a rapid boil; remove from heat. With the saucepan in one hand, let the boiling water dribble onto the cornmeal while stirring constantly with the other hand. Then stir the milk into the mixture (it will be fairly thick, but not runny).

Generously grease a large, heavy frying pan (I like to use my cast-iron frying pan) with the bacon drippings and heat. When pan is hot, drop the batter by spoonfuls. Flatten the batter with a spatula to a thickness of approximately 1/4 inch. Fry until golden brown, turn, and brown on the other side (adding more bacon drippings as needed).

Serve hot with butter, maple syrup, or applesauce.

Makes 4 servings.

> ### Bacon Fact:
> Roughly 11% of a standard pig's weight is made up of meat used for bacon.

SOUTH CAROLINA

SHRIMP and GRITS

INGREDIENTS

- 3 slices bacon, chopped
- Peanut oil, optional
- 1 pound medium shrimp, peeled and deveined
- 2 tbsp. flour
- 1 1/4 cups mushrooms, trimmed and sliced
- 1 large clove garlic, pressed
- 2 tsps. fresh lemon juice
- 1/2 tsp. hot sauce (Tabasco recommended)
- 1/4 cup scallions, thinly sliced
- Cooked grits, for serving

DIRECTIONS

In a medium skillet over low heat, cook the bacon, stirring occasionally, until crisp, about 8 minutes. Using a slotted spoon, transfer the bacon to a paper towel-lined plate and reserve the bacon fat. (Add enough peanut oil to the reserved bacon fat to amount to make 1 1/2 cups.) Reserve the skillet and fat.

In a medium bowl, toss the shrimp with flour until lightly coated. Heat the reserved skillet and fat over medium-high; cook shrimp until they begin to turn pink, about 1 minute. Stir in the mushrooms and reserved bacon; cook 1 minute. Stir in the garlic clove (do not let brown), about 30 seconds. Remove from the heat and stir in the lemon juice, hot sauce, and scallions. Serve immediately over cooked grits.

BACON-INFUSED CAROLINA FISH MUDDLE

INGREDIENTS

- 1 tsp. vegetable oil
- 1 pound wild American shrimp, peeled, deveined, shells reserved
- 8 sprigs thyme
- 4 bay leaves
- 2 28-ounce cans whole peeled tomatoes with juices
- 1 pound slab bacon, cut into 1/2" cubes, or thick-cut bacon, sliced into 1/2" strips
- 4 celery stalks, finely chopped
- 3 carrots, finely chopped
- 2 onions, finely chopped
- 1 leek (white and pale-green parts only), finely chopped
- 3 garlic cloves, finely chopped
- 1/2 jalapeño (with seeds), finely chopped
- 1 pound new potatoes, peeled, cut into 1/2" cubes
- Kosher salt, freshly ground pepper
- Hot pepper sauce (such as Cholula or Tabasco; optional)
- 1 pound black or striped bass fillet, cut into 1"-2" pieces
- 1 pound black or red grouper fillet, cut into 1"-2" pieces
- 6 slices baguette, toasted
- 6 cups cooked stone-ground grits or rice
- Chopped flat-leaf parsley

DIRECTIONS

Heat oil in a medium saucepan over medium heat. Add shrimp shells and cook, stirring constantly, until pink. Add 3 cups water and bring to a simmer. Cook gently until liquid is reduced to 2 cups. Strain stock, discarding shells. DO AHEAD: Can be made 1 day ahead. Cover and chill stock and shrimp separately.

Tie thyme sprigs and bay leaves into a bundle with kitchen twine; set aside. Pulse tomatoes with juices in a food processor until chunky purée forms; set aside. Heat bacon in a large Dutch oven over medium-low heat; cook, stirring occasionally, until some of fat is rendered and bacon is just beginning to crisp, 10-15 minutes. Using a slotted spoon, transfer bacon to paper towels to drain; reserve 2 tbsp. bacon drippings for croutons.

Add celery, carrots, onions, and leek to pot. Increase heat to medium and cook until vegetables are tender, about 10 minutes. Add garlic, jalapeño, and herb bundle; cook for 2 minutes. Add reserved tomato purée; cook, stirring often, for 20 minutes. Add shrimp stock (or, if omitting the first step, add 2 cups fish stock or clam juice) and bring to a simmer. Add potatoes and cooked bacon and simmer until potatoes are tender, about 15 minutes. Season stew with salt, pepper, and hot pepper sauce, if desired.

Add fish and shrimp; bring to a gentle simmer. Cover; cook until fish and shrimp are just opaque in center, about 5 minutes.

Meanwhile, brush bacon fat onto toast to make croutons. Ladle muddle into bowls over grits or rice, sprinkle with parsley, and garnish each bowl with a crouton.

Bacon Fact:

Bacon-related menu items have grown by more than 7% annually in the last few years.

SOUTH DAKOTA

CHISLIC (SOUTH DAKOTA CUBED MEAT)

INGREDIENTS

- 1 pound boneless lamb leg, cut into 1-inch cubes
- Bacon as needed
- 1 1/2 tsps. Worcestershire sauce
- 3/4 tsp. chili powder
- 3/4 tsp. kosher salt
- 1/2 tsp. garlic powder
- 1/2 tsp. onion powder
- 1/4 tsp. ground black pepper
- Vegetable oil, for frying
- Serving suggestions: garlic salt, hot sauce and saltine crackers
- Special equipment: Toothpicks, for serving

DIRECTIONS

Toss together the lamb cubes, Worcestershire sauce, chili powder, salt, garlic powder, onion powder and pepper in a bowl. Marinate in the refrigerator for 1 hour.

Heat 2 inches of oil in a Dutch oven to 375 degrees F. Wrap each cube in bacon. Fry the marinated lamb cubes in batches to avoid overcrowding the oil. Cook to medium-rare, about 1 minute. The meat will have a dark brown crust and will be tender to the touch. Drain on a paper-towel-lined plate. Skewer the lamb cubes with toothpicks and serve with garlic salt, hot sauce and saltine crackers on the side.

CREAMY SOUTH DAKOTA PHEASANT

INGREDIENTS

6 pheasant breast fillets

1/2 cup flour

1/2 cup milk or cream

salt & pepper to taste

1/4 cup Crisco or vegetable oil (less if you like)

1 sm. can cream of chicken or mushroom soup

(gravy lovers double this)

DIRECTIONS

Combine flour, salt, & pepper. Coat breasts with flour mixture. Brown floured fillets in heated Crisco until golden on both sides. Place fillets in greased baking dish in single layer. Combine soup & milk to pour over browned fillets. Bake covered 2 hours at 325°F. Serve with mashed potatoes, and you'll have enough gravy to use on potatoes.

Bacon Fact:
The firmer the fat the less bacon will curl as it cooks.

TENNESSEE

MEMPHIS BACON DRY RUB RIBS

INGREDIENTS

MEMPHIS DRY RUB

- 3 tbsp. dark brown sugar
- 1 1/2 tbsp. kosher salt
- 1 tbsp. ground coriander
- 1 tbsp. mustard powder
- 1 tbsp. onion powder
- 1 tbsp. Spanish paprika
- 2 tsps. garlic powder
- 2 tsps. ground black pepper
- 1 tsp. cayenne
- 2 racks pork ribs (about 2 1/2 pounds per rack)
- 1 cup apple cider
- 1/2 cup apple cider vinegar
- 1/8 cup dark brown sugar

DIRECTIONS

For the rub: Mix together the brown sugar, salt, coriander, mustard powder, onion powder, paprika, garlic powder, black pepper and cayenne.

Remove the thin membrane on the back of each rib by placing the ribs on the counter with the underside facing up. Slip a small knife between the bone and the membrane. Once enough membrane is released, gently pull it free from the bones. Use a dish towel to get a secure grip.

Place the ribs on a foil-lined baking sheet and rub both sides of the ribs with the dry rub. Wrap ribs in as much bacon as you want. Cover with plastic wrap and let marinate in the fridge for a minimum of 3 hours, preferably overnight.

Preheat the oven to 300 degrees F. Bring the ribs to room temperature and place bone-side up on the baking sheet. Pour the apple cider around the ribs and place another piece of foil over top, forming a packet. Crimp the ends of the two pieces of foil tightly together to seal completely. Place in the oven and cook for 2 hours. Remove the top foil and turn the ribs over. Raise the oven temperature to 375 degrees F and cook until the ribs develop a rich dark bark, the edges are crisp and the meat is fork tender, 30 to 45 minutes.

In a small saucepan, add the apple cider vinegar and brown sugar. Bring to a boil and then reduce to simmer until a loose glaze forms, about 3 minutes. Glaze your ribs with this when they come out of the oven. Transfer to a cutting board, cut and serve.

PRALINE BACON

INGREDIENTS

- 1 lb. Krause's Double smoked Bacon, thick sliced
- 4 tbsp. Cane Syrup or Corn Syrup
- 3/4 Cup Brown Sugar
- 3/4 Cup Pecans, toasted and chopped

DIRECTIONS

Preheat the oven to 400 degrees F.

Place a wire rack on a sheet tray. Combine the Pecans and brown sugar. Lay the bacon side by side on the rack, place in the preheated oven for about 15-20 minutes, or until the bacon is sizzling and starting to brown around the edges. The object is for the bacon to cook about 3/4 of the way through before adding the topping.

Push the partially cooked bacon as close together as possible on the rack and brush with the cane syrup, this will give the topping something to grab on to. Cover generously with the Pecan/brown sugar topping. Place back in the oven for about 10 minutes more or until the topping is bubbly and the bacon is good and brown. Let cool.

As the Praline Bacon cools it will set up and have a nice chewy bite to it.

Serves 4 as a side.

> **Bacon Fact:**
> Hungarians have been known to roast their bacon on a stick and catch the fat drippings on a slice of bread for consumption.

TEXAS

TEXAS BRISKET with BACON LATTICE

INGREDIENTS

- 6 pounds beef brisket
- 1-2 packages of bacon
- 1 tbsp. yellow mustard
- 1/4 cup dark brown sugar
- 3/4 cup paprika
- 2 tbsp. chipotle chili powder
- 1/4 cup black pepper
- 2 tbsp. garlic powder
- 1/4 cup salt
- 2 tbsp. onion powder
- 1 tbsp. cayenne pepper

DIRECTIONS

Trim the fat cap on the brisket to about 1/4 to 1/8 of an inch. Coat the brisket with a light coating of the yellow mustard. Mix the sugar and spices together to form the rub for the brisket. Apply the rub to both sides of the meat. Wrap entire brisket in a bacon lattice weaving each strip carefully around the brisket.

Place the brisket in a preheated 194 to 205 degree F smoker until the meat reaches an internal temperature of 185 to 195 degrees F, about 1 1/2 hours per pound. Once the internal temperature is reached, remove the brisket from the smoker and allow it to rest for at least 30 minutes before slicing.

TEXAS STYLE BACON, BEANS and EGGS: BLACK BEAN CHILAQUILES

INGREDIENTS

- 12 corn or flour tortillas, cut into strips
- Cooking spray
- 1 tbsp. vegetable oil
- 8 slices smoky lean bacon, sliced across the strips 1/2-inch long
- 1 red onion, peeled, quartered and sliced
- 2 Fresno or jalapeno chiles, sliced
- 4 cloves garlic, chopped
- 1 (28-ounce) can black beans
- 1 tbsp. cumin (a scant palmful)
- 1 rounded tbsp. chile powder (a healthy palmful)
- Salt and freshly ground black pepper
- 1 cup beer
- 1 (14-ounce) can diced fire-roasted tomatoes
- Small handful fresh cilantro leaves, chopped
- 1 1/2 to 2 cups shredded hot pepper sharp Cheddar cheese or Pepper Jack cheese
- 4 eggs, to prepare any style (1 per person)
- Ripe avocado, halved, pitted and diced
- Lime, cut into wedges

DIRECTIONS

Preheat oven to 425 degrees F.

Cut tortillas into strips and spray with cooking spray. Bake 12 to 15 minutes until crisp. Arrange in casserole dish.

Heat a skillet over medium-high heat with 1 tablespoon vegetable oil. Add bacon and brown then remove with a slotted spoon. To the skillet, add the onions, Fresno peppers, and garlic and sauté a few minutes.

Add the beans and season with cumin, chile powder, salt, and pepper, stir in tomatoes, cilantro, and beer. Thicken 1 minute, then adjust seasoning and arrange on top of tortillas, and scatter in bacon bits and cheese.

Cool and store for make-ahead meal.

Bake in the hot oven until bubbly and hot, top with fried eggs (as soft or hard as you like), diced avocado and lime wedges.

Bacon Fact:

Proscuitto is gourmet Italian bacon that has been dry-cured, aged and spiced.

UTAH

UTAH POTATO BACON CASSEROLE

INGREDIENTS

- 4 tbsp. unsalted butter
- 1 small onion, diced (about 1 cup)
- 2 cloves garlic, minced
- One 30-ounce bag frozen shredded hash brown potatoes, lightly thawed
- One 10.5-ounce can condensed cream of chicken soup
- 1 cup sour cream
- 1/2 cup of bacon crumble
- 1/4 cup grated Parmesan
- 1 1/2 tsps. kosher salt
- 1/2 tsp. ground black pepper
- 2 cups shredded sharp yellow Cheddar
- 1 1/2 cups lightly crushed corn flake cereal

DIRECTIONS

Preheat the oven to 350 degrees F.

Heat 2 tbsp butter over medium heat in a skillet. Add the diced onion and cook, stirring, until soft and translucent, about 6 minutes. Stir in the garlic and cook until fragrant and softened, an additional 2 minutes.

In a bowl, toss together the cooked onions and garlic, hash brown potatoes, condensed soup, sour cream, bacon crumble, Parmesan, salt, pepper and 1 1/2 cups Cheddar. Spread the mixture in a 9-by-13 inch casserole dish. Melt the remaining 2 tbsp butter. Top the casserole with the remaining 1/2 cup cheese, corn flake cereal and melted butter.

Bake in the oven until it bubbles around the sides, about 1 hour.

BACON and CHEESE WAFFLES

INGREDIENTS

- 2 cups pancake or biscuit/baking mix
- 1 egg
- 1 cup 2% milk
- 1 cup (8 ounces) sour cream
- 1 tbsp. butter, melted
- 6 to 8 bacon strips, cooked and crumbled
- 1 cup (4 ounces) shredded cheddar cheese

DIRECTIONS

Place pancake mix in a large bowl. In another bowl, whisk the egg milk, sour cream and butter. Stir into pancake mix until blended. Fold in bacon and cheese.

Bake in a preheated waffle iron according to manufacturer's directions until golden brown. Yield: 12 waffles (4-inch square).

Bacon Fact:

The foodservice market uses more than 1.7 billion pounds of bacon each year.

VERMONT

BACON CHEDDAR CHEESE APPLE PIE

INGREDIENTS

CRUST:

- 2 1/2 cups all-purpose flour, plus extra for dusting
- 2 tsps. sugar
- 1 tsp. salt
- 1/2 cup shortening
- 1 stick cold unsalted butter, cut into 1/4-inch dice
- 1 cup shredded white or yellow Cheddar, cold
- 2-3 slices of crispy bacon crumble
- 1 tsp. apple cider vinegar
- 3 to 4 tbsp. ice water
- 1 large egg

FILLING:

- 6 tbsp. unsalted butter
- 6 Cortland apples (about 2 1/2 pounds), peeled and sliced 1/4-inch thick
- 6 Granny Smith apples (about 2 1/2 pounds), peeled and sliced 1/4-inch thick
- 1 cup sugar
- 1 tsp. lemon zest
- 1 tbsp. lemon juice

- 3/4 tsp. ground cinnamon
- 1/4 tsp. ground nutmeg
- Pinch of salt
- 3 tbsp. all-purpose flour
- Special equipment: 9 1/2-inch deep-dish pie plate

DIRECTIONS

For the crust: Put the flour, sugar and salt in the bowl of a food processor. Pulse a couple of times to mix. Add the shortening and pulse to combine. Add the butter and pulse until the mixture is coarse and a few pieces of butter are still visible. Add the bacon, cheese and pulse just to combine. Add the apple cider vinegar and ice water. Pulse until the dough just begins to come together; it should look moist but still crumbly and not yet a complete ball. Turn the dough out onto a piece of plastic wrap and quickly form into a ball. Divide into 2 disks, one slightly larger than the other, wrap in plastic and refrigerate 1 hour or overnight. The less you work the dough the flakier it will be.

For the filling: Melt the butter in a large skillet over medium heat. Once melted, add the apples (if the apples cannot sit in one even layer, use 2 medium saute pans to cook the apples in batches). Add the sugar, lemon zest, lemon juice, cinnamon, nutmeg and salt. Continue cooking over medium heat until the apples release their liquid and it begins to boil, 12 to 15 minutes. The apples will be tender but will not lose their shape. Once the apples are tender, add the flour and cook until the liquid has thickened and coats the back of a spoon, about 1 minute longer. Remove the apples to a baking sheet and spread out in an even layer to cool to room temperature, about 1 hour.

Preheat the oven to 425 degrees F. Place a baking sheet in the oven while preheating so it will be hot by the time the pie goes into the oven.

Roll the larger disk of dough on a lightly floured surface to about 12 inches in diameter and 1/8-inch thick, to fit a 9 1/2-inch deep-dish pie plate. Roll the dough onto your rolling pin and then unroll it over your pie plate. Trim the excess dough to 1/2-inch, and do not crimp the edges. Place the cooled filling in the pie plate, mounding at the center.

Roll the smaller disk of dough on a lightly floured surface to 1/8-inch thick and 10 inches in diameter and place on top of the filling. Fold the edges under, and decoratively crimp the edges. Cut slits in the top crust to allow steam to escape. Whisk the egg with 1 tsp water and brush the top of the pie.

Place the pie on the preheated baking sheet and bake for 10 minutes. Decrease the temperature to 350 degrees F and continue baking until the top crust is golden brown and crisp to the touch and the bottom crust is browned, 50 to 60 minutes. Cool to room temperature and serve.

VERMONT BAKED BEANS

INGREDIENTS

- 1 pound dried navy beans
- 4 cups water
- 1/2 pound thick-sliced bacon strips, chopped
- 1 large onion, chopped
- 2/3 cup maple syrup
- 2 tsp. salt
- 1 tsp. ground mustard
- 1/2 tsp. coarsely ground pepper

DIRECTIONS

Soak beans according to package directions. Drain and rinse beans, discarding liquid. Return beans to Dutch oven; add water. Bring to a boil.

Meanwhile, in a large skillet, cook bacon over medium heat until crisp; drain. Stir the onion, syrup, salt, mustard, pepper and bacon into the beans.

Cover and bake at 300° for 3 to 3-1/2 hours or until beans are tender and reach desired consistency, stirring every 30 minutes. Yield: 8 servings.

Bacon Fact:

Another word for Canadian bacon is Peameal bacon.

VIRGINIA

VIRGINIA HAM BACON BISCUITS

INGREDIENTS

- 3 cups all-purpose flour, plus more for dusting
- 1 tbsp. baking powder
- 1 1/2 tsps. kosher salt
- 1 tsp. baking soda
- 2 tbsp. chopped fresh chives
- 8 tbsp. cold lard, cut into small chunks
- 1 1/2 cups buttermilk
- 1/4 cup whole grain mustard
- 1 tbsp. honey
- 1 tsp. Dijon mustard
- 8 ounces ham, sliced 1/4-inch thick, from a bone-in or boneless ham
- 24 cooked bacon slices

DIRECTIONS

Preheat the oven to 400 degrees F. In a large bowl, whisk together the flour, baking powder, salt, baking soda and chives. Using a pastry blender or your hands, cut in the lard until the mixture resembles coarse crumbs. Make a well in the center and pour in the buttermilk. Mix gently until a soft dough forms.

Turn the dough out onto a lightly floured surface and knead about 5 times. Roll out to 1-inch thick. Cut out using a 2 1/2-inch cutter. Reroll the scraps and cut out the rest. Place on an ungreased baking sheet and bake until the biscuits are puffed and golden brown, about 20 minutes.

In a small bowl, whisk the whole grain mustard, honey and Dijon mustard until smooth.

When the biscuits are cool enough to handle, split and spread the bottoms with the honey mustard. Add the ham, two bacon slices and the biscuit top. Serve warm or at room temperature.

SCALLOPED OYSTERS WITH BACON

INGREDIENTS

- 1 qt. shucked oysters
- 3 strips bacon, crisped and broken in bits
- Fat from bacon
- 2 tbsp. butter
- 1 box soda crackers
- Pepper and salt

DIRECTIONS

Drain oysters. Save their liquor. Preheat oven to 425°. Season oysters to taste with pepper and salt. In a deep baking pan, put a layer of oysters, then a layer of coarsely crushed crackers, sprinkle with bits of bacon and add a little of the fat and bits of butter. Alternate layers, until pan is nearly full. Add oyster liquor. Cook until oysters are set and brown on top. 10 to 12 minutes.

Bacon Fact:
3 slices of cooked bacon contains about 100 calories.

WASHINGTON

PLANKED SALMON with HONEY-BALSAMIC GLAZE WRAPPED in BACON

INGREDIENTS

- 1 whole side of salmon, or 4 (6-ounce) salmon fillets
- 20 slices of bacon
- 1 tbsp. fine sea salt, preferably gray salt
- 1/2 tsp. freshly ground black pepper
- 1/4 tsp. dry mustard
- 1/2 cup honey
- 1/4 cup balsamic vinegar
- Melted butter, for brushing salmon
- 2 untreated cedar planks, each about 5 by 12-inches, soaked in water to cover for at least 12 hours (available at hardware stores)
- Extra-virgin olive oil, for oiling the planks

DIRECTIONS

Preheat the broiler. Preheat the oven to 400 degrees F.

If using a side of salmon, cut about halfway through the flesh about every 5 to 6-inches so there are some spaces for the glazes to sink in. If using salmon fillets, slice about 8 to 10 sliced angles into flesh, to help flesh more completely soak in the glaze.

In a small bowl or cup, mix the salt, pepper, and dry mustard.

In a medium glass bowl, heat the honey in the microwave for 30 seconds to liquefy further. Remove from the microwave and mix in balsamic vinegar.

Brush the top of the salmon fillets (not the skin side) with the melted butter. Season the flesh side with the spice mixture. Brush with the honey-balsamic mixture, reserving some for later.

Put the soaked planks under the hot broiler, about 5 inches from the heat source, until the wood is browned on top, about 3 minutes. With tongs, carefully remove the planks from the oven.

Immediately brush the browned surface with olive oil, then lay the salmon fillets on the oiled surface, skin side down.

Put 2 cookie sheets in the oven below where the planks will go to catch any glazes or juices that run off. Return the planks to the broiler and cook the fish for 10 minutes. Wrap each fillet with two slices of bacon. Baste with honey-balsamic and place in oven. Cook until it is done to your taste, about 10 to 15 more minutes, or 20 minutes total for medium.

Remove the fillets to a platter, or immediately serve directly from the planks.

PANCETTA BACON PASTA

INGREDIENTS

- 1 tbsp. clarified butter
- 1 pound 4 ounces Pancetta, diced, recipe follows
- 1 tsp. finely diced garlic
- 1/4 cup white wine
- 5 ounces heavy cream
- Cooked pasta, for serving
- 1/4 cup finely grated Parmesan, plus more for serving
- 1/4 tsp. ground white pepper
- 1/4 tsp. salt

PANCETTA:

- 5 pounds fresh pork belly
- 2 tsp. pink salt
- 2 ounces kosher salt
- 2 1/2 tbsp. brown sugar
- 4 tbsp. ground black pepper
- 1 tbsp. ground white pepper, plus more for dusting
- 2 tbsp. juniper berries, cracked
- 5 bay leaves, crumbled small
- 1 tsp. ground nutmeg
- 1/4 tsp. ground allspice
- 1 tbsp. dried thyme leaves
- 2 tbsp. pureed fresh garlic
- 5 sprigs fresh thyme

DIRECTIONS

Heat the butter in a large saute pan. Add the Pancetta and saute until slightly brown. Add the garlic, saute briefly, and then deglaze with the wine. Reduce the wine by half, and then add the heavy cream. Reduce this by one third, and then toss in your cooked pasta. Heat the pasta through and add the Parmesan, white pepper, and salt and toss. Pour into bowls and add more Parmesan cheese (as much as you like).

PANCETTA:

Ask your butcher for a 5 pound, nice square piece of pork belly (skinless) that will fit into a 2-gallon zip-top bag.

Pat the belly with paper towels to dry. Mix together all the spices. Wearing plastic gloves, rub the cure mixture into both sides of the belly. Place in a 2-gallon zip-top bag, put on a sheet pan, and refrigerate. Every day for 1 week, turn the bag over and massage the belly (through the bag) to ensure saturation. The pork will take on a slightly darker color than what it was. This is a sign that the cure is working. It will also draw some moisture out of the belly. When the meat is darker and firmer, remove the belly from the bag and run under water to remove any cure sediment. Pat dry and lightly cover with a dusting of ground white pepper. Roll the belly very tightly into a log and wrap tightly with cheesecloth. Tie the end and hang in a 34 to 38 degree F refrigerator for at least 2 weeks. At this time the bacon should be fully cured and have a good firmness when squeezed.

Bacon Fact:

Almost half of the fat in bacon is the "good fat" that can actually help lower bad cholesterol.

WEST VIRGINIA

WEST VIRGINIA BACON PEPPERONI ROLL

INGREDIENTS

- 1 1/2 cups milk
- 8 slices of bacon
- 3 tbsp. unsalted butter
- 2 tbsp. sugar
- 2 tsps. kosher salt
- 2 tsps. active dry yeast (1 packet)
- 3 1/2 cups all-purpose flour, plus more for dusting
- 1 large egg
- One 6-ounce stick pepperoni, cut into 4 logs and each split in half lengthwise
- 1/4 cup extra-virgin olive oil
- 1 1/2 cups shredded whole milk mozzarella

DIRECTIONS

In a small saucepan, gently heat the milk and butter until the butter is melted. The milk should be just a little hotter than warm, between 100 and 115 degrees F, but not over 115 degrees F. Remove the saucepan from the heat and whisk in the sugar, salt and yeast. Let the mixture sit until the yeast is activated and foam covers the top, 5 to 8 minutes.

Add the flour to a large bowl and make a well in the center. Crack the egg into the middle and pour in the yeast liquid. Make the dough by mixing all ingredients together with a rubber spatula. Make sure all ingredients are incorporated; the dough will be sticky and loose. Leave the dough in the center of the bowl when it is fully incorporated. Cover the bowl with plastic wrap and let rise in a warm place until doubled in size, about 2 hours. Remove the plastic and gently re-knead the dough while still in the bowl. Form into a ball, as best you can, and cover with plastic wrap. This time allow to rest in a warm place for 1 hour.

After the second rise, remove the dough to a very generously floured surface, kneading to bring together. Cut the dough into 8 pieces, about 3 1/2 ounces each. Gently form each piece of dough into balls, incorporating more flour as needed. Use your hands to flatten each ball to a 4 1/2-inch circle. Wrap each piece of pepperoni with bacon. Brush a piece of pepperoni with oil and place in the center of the circle, along with 2 tbsp shredded mozzarella. Fold the dough over the pepperoni, like a burrito, and place on a parchment-covered baking sheet seam side down. Repeat with the remaining pepperoni and cheese. As you place each pepperoni roll on the sheet tray, leave at least 1 inch or space around each roll to allow for a third rise (therefore you will need 2 baking sheets). Cover the rolls loosely with plastic wrap and place in a warm place for 30 minutes. The rolls will puff up just a bit.

Preheat the oven to 350 degrees F. Brush the tops of rolls with the remaining oil and bake in the oven 30 to 35 minutes. The rolls will have a rich golden color and crispy crust.

Cook's Note: This dough is very wet, and will look too loose when you first make it. Use a rubber spatula when incorporating flour into the dough. Make sure to always flour your hands and the surface you are working on when working with the dough.

RAMPS with POTATOES and EGGS

INGREDIENTS:

- 6 slices bacon cooked and chopped
- 1 cup ramps, white parts and leaves
- chopped 2-3 medium size potatoes, peeled and chopped
- 5 large eggs
- salt
- pepper
- chives
- shredded cheese

DIRECTIONS

Cook bacon in a large frying pan, remove, drain, and chop it up, then set aside. Using the same pan with the bacon grease, fry ramps and potatoes over low heat, covered, until the potatoes are soft. Crack the eggs over the ramps and potatoes mixture and fry, covered, until the eggs are done to however you like them. Sprinkle on some shredded Cheddar. Season with salt, pepper, and chives to taste. Serve immediately and top with the chopped bacon.

Bacon Fact:
Beef, turkey, chicken, lamb, and even goat may be used to make bacon.

WISCONSIN

BRATWURST STEWED with SAUERKRAUT and WRAPPED in BACON

INGREDIENTS

- 2 tbsp. oil
- 2 pounds fresh bratwurst links
- 2 packages of bacon
- 2 onions, chopped
- 2 garlic cloves, minced
- 3 cups chicken stock
- 1 tbsp. paprika
- 1 tbsp. caraway seed
- 4 cups sauerkraut, drained
- 2 tbsp. chopped fresh dill
- 1 baguette

DIRECTIONS

In a large pan, heat oil over high heat. Wrap each bratwurst with up to three slices of bacon. Brown bratwurst in oil and reduce heat to medium. Add onions and garlic and cook until lightly caramelized. Add stock, paprika, caraway seeds, and sauerkraut and simmer for 45 minutes. Remove from heat and stir in fresh dill. Serve on baguette.

BACON MAC & CHEESE with WISCONSIN GRUYÈRE

INGREDIENTS

- 1 quart (4 cups) heavy cream
- ½ tbsp. fresh rosemary, chopped
- Salt and cracked black pepper to taste
- ½ pound bacon, diced, fried crisp and drained
- 1 pound elbow macaroni or short hollow pasta, cooked according
- to package directions and drained, reserving 3 teaspoons pasta water
- 2 cups (8 ounces) Wisconsin Gruyère cheese, grated
- Chopped chives for garnish

DIRECTIONS

Place cream in large saucepan with rosemary.

Add salt and pepper.

Bring to boil and keep at boil until reduced by half (be patient, this takes some time).

Stir in bacon and pasta and simmer until hot; add cheese and 3 teaspoons pasta water. Stir until cheese is melted. Garnish with chopped chives. Serve immediately.

Bacon Fact:
The B.L.T. name came from a waitress who would use shorthand to speed up orders.

WYOMING

CHICKEN FRIED STEAK with BACON and CREAM GRAVY

INGREDIENTS

STEAK:

- 3 pounds (about 6 ounces each) rib eye steaks, 1/2-inch thick
- 3/4 cup milk
- 1 egg, beaten
- 2 to 3 cups flour
- 2 tsps. seasoning salt
- 1 tsp. freshly ground black pepper
- Canola oil

CREAM GRAVY:

- 10 crispy slices of bacon, crumbled
- 3 heaping tbsp. flour
- 2 cups cold milk
- Kosher salt and freshly ground black pepper

DIRECTIONS

For the steak: Trim any remaining fat off the steaks and, using a mallet or rolling pin, pound out the steaks to 1/4-inch thick.

Beat together the milk and egg in a shallow dish and set aside. Place the flour in a shallow dish, season well with the seasoning salt and pepper and set aside.

Cover the bottom of a large skillet, preferably cast iron, with enough oil to reach about 1/2-inch up the pan. Heat over medium-high heat.

Coat the steaks in the egg mixture, then the flour and then add to the pan. Cook until the juices begin to surface and the bottom is nice and brown, 2 to 3 minutes. Flip the steaks and cook another 2 to 3 minutes more. Be careful to not overcook. Continue this process until all the steaks are cooked, placing the finished steaks on a paper towel-lined baking sheet.

After frying the steaks, prepare to make the gravy: Let the drippings in the pan sit until the excess browned bits of seasoning settle to the bottom of the skillet. Pour off most of the oil, leaving about 4 tbsp behind with the brown bits. Add the flour, stirring until well mixed. Place the skillet back over medium-high heat and slowly add the milk while stirring constantly. Add bacon crumble. Cook until the gravy comes to a boil. Season with salt and pepper. Serve with chicken fried steak.

WYOMING LAMB STEW

INGREDIENTS

- 5 bacon strips, diced
- 1/4 cup all-purpose flour
- 1 tsp. salt
- 1/2 tsp. pepper
- 6 lamb shanks (about 6 pounds)
- 1 can (28 ounces) diced tomatoes, undrained
- 1 can (14-1/2 ounces) beef broth
- 1 can (8 ounces) tomato sauce

- 2 cans (4 ounces each) mushroom stems and pieces, drained
- 2 medium onions, chopped
- 1 cup chopped celery
- 1/2 cup minced fresh parsley
- 2 tbsp. prepared horseradish
- 1 tbsp. cider vinegar
- 2 tsp. Worcestershire sauce
- 1 garlic clove, minced

DIRECTIONS

In a Dutch oven, cook bacon over medium heat until crisp. Using a slotted spoon, remove to paper towels to drain, reserving drippings. Reserve bacon for garnish; refrigerate.

In a large resealable plastic bag, combine the flour, salt and pepper; add lamb shanks, one at a time and shake to coat. In bacon drippings, brown shanks on all sides; drain. Add the remaining ingredients. Bring to a boil.

Cover and bake at 325° for 2 to 2-1/2 hours or until the meat is very tender; skim fat. Garnish with bacon. Yield: 6 servings.

Bacon Fact:

Serrano is Spanish bacon very similar to Proscuitto.

OTHER BOOKS

Need extra money but don't know where to start? Tired of losing money to expenses and liabilities and have no money to save? Tired of get rich quick scams that take your money? Learn 18 guaranteed tip$ that will put more money in your pockets!

Available on Kindle at Amazon.com

Ever wonder why you're not rich or financially secure? In, Let Them Eat Cash, you'll find out what you're doing wrong and find out how to fix. Learn what the Middle Class is doing wrong, what the rich think about it, what the rich do differently, and techniques which will help you start you on a path to becoming financially secure!

Available on Kindle at Amazon.com

NOTES

"8 Mouth-Watering Recipes For West Virginia Ramps That'll Make You So Hungry." Only In Your State. Web. 31 May 2015.

"Alabama Recipes." Alabama Living Magazine. Web. 28 Feb. 2015. <http://alabamaliving.coop/article/alabama-recipes-6/>.

"Bacon and Cheese Waffles." Taste of Home. Web. 31 May 2015.

"Bacon Mac & Cheese with Wisconsin Gruyère." Easy Recipes Tips Ideas and Life Musings. Web. 31 May 2015.

"Bacon Guacamole Recipe." KTVK Azfamily.com. Web. 28 Feb. 2015. <http://www.azfamily.com/good-morning-arizona/Bacon-Guacamole-259115621.html>.

"Baked Halibut Supreme." Recipe with Wild Alaska Halibut. Web. 28 Feb. 2015. <http://www.great-alaska-seafood.com/recipes/baked-halibut-supreme-recipe.htm>.

"Bacon & Cheddar Deviled Eggs." Bacon & Cheddar Deviled Eggs. Web. 28 Feb. 2015. <http://www.coloradoeggproducers.com/recipe/simply-eggs/bacon-amp-cheddar-deviled-eggs>.

"Bacon Cheddar Mashed Potatoes | Recipe on Idahopotato.com." Idaho Potato Recipes. Web. 1 Mar. 2015. <http://recipes.idahopotato.com/bacon-cheddar-mashed-potatoes/>.

"Bacon Cinnamon Rolls | Plain Chicken." Bacon Cinnamon Rolls | Plain Chicken. Web. 28 Feb. 2015. <http://www.plainchicken.com/2010/11/bacon-cinnamon-rolls.html>.

"Bacon and Smoked Gouda Pizza | The Home Pizzeria." The Home Pizzeria. 4 June 2013. Web. 14 Mar. 2015. <http://www.thehomepizzeria.com/recipes/pizza-toppings/bacon-and-smoked-gouda-pizza/#>.

"Bacon Peach Cobbler." Bacon Peach Cobbler. Web. 28 Feb. 2015. <http://fastpaleo.com/recipe/bacon-peach-cobbler/>.

"Bacon Wrapped Alaska Scallops Recipe - Food.com." Bacon Wrapped Alaska Scallops Recipe - Food.com. Web. 28 Feb. 2015. <http://www.food.com/recipe/bacon-wrapped-alaska-scallops-108565>.

"Bacon Wrapped Alaska Scallop Sliders." Bacon Wrapped Alaska Scallop Sliders. Web. 28 Feb. 2015. <http://www.copperriverseafoods.com/bacon-wrapped-alaska-scallop-sliders/>.

"Bacon-Wrapped Mini Meatloaves | Paleo Leap." Paleo Leap Paleo Diet Recipes Tips. 4 Feb. 2013. Web. 28 Feb. 2015. <http://paleoleap.com/bacon-wrapped-mini-meatloaves/>.

"Bacon-Wrapped Seafood Skewers." Taste of Home. Web. 31 May 2015. <http://www.tasteofhome.com/recipes/bacon-wrapped-seafood-skewers>.

"Barbeque Bacon Chicken Bake." Allrecipes.com. Web. 1 Mar. 2015. <http://allrecipes.com/recipe/barbeque-bacon-chicken-bake/>.

"Beef Stew with Bacon." Williams-Sonoma. Web. 31 May 2015.

"Bratwurst Stewed with Sauerkraut : Recipes : Cooking Channel."
    Bratwurst Stewed with Sauerkraut : Recipes : Cooking
    Channel. Web. 15 Mar. 2015.
    <http://www.cookingchanneltv.com/recipes/michael-
    symon/bratwurst-stewed-with-sauerkraut.html>.

"Bubba's Jambalaya." Allrecipes.com. Web. 7 Mar. 2015.
    <http://allrecipes.com/recipe/bubbas-jambalaya/>.

"California Roll Breakfast Sushi - #TopChef - Farmgirl Gourmet."
    Farmgirl Gourmet. 26 Jan. 2013. Web. 28 Feb. 2015.
    <http://www.farmgirlgourmet.com/2013/01/california-sushi-
    roll.html>.

"Cheddar Bacon Chicken Tenders." Bettycrocker.com. Web. 28 Feb.
    2015. <http://www.bettycrocker.com/recipes/cheddar-bacon-
    chicken-tenders/846d3996-ecce-47e3-a13f-bba6b7db87ba>.

"Cheddar Cheese Apple Pie : Recipes : Cooking Channel." Cheddar
    Cheese Apple Pie : Recipes : Cooking Channel. Web. 15 Mar.
    2015. <http://www.cookingchanneltv.com/recipes/cheddar-
    cheese-apple-pie.html>.

"Cheesy Bacon Bombs!" Oh Bite It. Web. 15 Mar. 2015.
    <http://www.ohbiteit.com/2013/04/cheesy-bacon-
    bombs.html>.

"Chicken Fried Steak with Cream Gravy : Recipes : Cooking
    Channel." Chicken Fried Steak with Cream Gravy : Recipes :
    Cooking Channel. Web. 15 Mar. 2015.
    <http://www.cookingchanneltv.com/recipes/chicken-fried-
    steak-with-cream-gravy.html>.

"Chislic (South Dakota Cubed Meat) : Recipes : Cooking Channel."
Chislic (South Dakota Cubed Meat) : Recipes : Cooking
Channel. Web. 15 Mar. 2015.
<http://www.cookingchanneltv.com/recipes/chislic-south-
dakota-cubed-meat.html>.

"Creamy Bacon-Mushroom Shrimp and Grits." / Entrees / Recipes /
Home. Web. 28 Feb. 2015.
<http://www.freshfromflorida.com/Recipes/Entrees/Creamy-
Bacon-Mushroom-Shrimp-and-Grits>.

"Crispy Cornmeal Okra : Recipes : Cooking Channel." Crispy
Cornmeal Okra : Recipes : Cooking Channel. Web. 15 Mar.
2015. <http://www.cookingchanneltv.com/recipes/crispy-
cornmeal-okra.html>.

"Danger Dogs Bacon Wrapped Hot Dogs Recipe." Bacon Freak. Web.
14 Mar. 2015. <http://www.baconfreak.com/recipe-danger-
dogs.html>.

"Delaware Creamed Succotash from Leite's Culinaria." Leites
Culinaria. Web. 28 Feb. 2015.
<http://leitesculinaria.com/7315/recipes-delaware-creamed-
succotash.html>.

"Eat at Home Alabama." Eat at Home Alabama. Web. 28 Feb. 2015.
<http://www.citationmachine.net/mla/cite-a-website/edit>.

"Fried Ravioli : Recipes : Cooking Channel." Fried Ravioli : Recipes :
Cooking Channel. Web. 23 Mar. 2015.
<http://www.cookingchanneltv.com/recipes/fried-
ravioli.html>.

"Funeral Potatoes Recipe : Cooking Channel." Funeral Potatoes
Recipe : Cooking Channel. Web. 15 Mar. 2015.

<http://www.cookingchanneltv.com/recipes/funeral-potatoes-utah-potato-casserole.html>.

"Hamburger Recipe -A Happy Camper-Idaho Bacon Burgers." Hamburger Recipe -A Happy Camper-Idaho Bacon Burgers. Web. 1 Mar. 2015. <http://ahappycamper.com/products/dorecipes/beef/bacon-burgers.html>.

"Hawaiian BBQ Bacon Cheeseburger - The Cozy Cook." The Cozy Cook. 1 July 2014. Web. 1 Mar. 2015. <http://thecozycook.com/hawaiian-bbq-bacon-cheeseburger/>.

"Homegrown Recipe: Colorado Sweet Corn Bacon Salsa and Corncakes - Aurora Sentinel." Aurora Sentinel. 1 Aug. 2012. Web. 28 Feb. 2015. <http://www.aurorasentinel.com/guide/colorado-table/homegrown-recipe-colorado-sweet-corn-bacon-salsa-and-corncakes/>.

"JohnnycakesJohnnycake History and Recipe." Johnnycake History and Recipe, Shawnee Cakes, Whats Cooking America. Web. 31 May 2015.

"Killer Griller: Double Onion Bacon Burger Recipe from Marcia Selden Catering." OmNomCT. 22 May 2014. Web. 28 Feb. 2015. <https://omnomct.wordpress.com/2014/05/22/killer-griller-double-onion-bacon-burger-recipe-from-marcia-selden-catering/>.

"Make My Sushi." Make My Sushi. Web. 28 Feb. 2015. <http://makemysushi.com/Recipes/epic-sushi-roll-with-bacon.html>.

"Maple Bacon Monkey Bread." Allrecipes.com. Web. 1 Mar. 2015.
<http://allrecipes.com/recipe/maple-bacon-monkey-bread/>.

"Maple Bourbon Bacon Jam." Closet Cooking. Web. 7 Mar. 2015.
<http://www.closetcooking.com/2012/08/maple-bourbon-bacon-jam.html>.

"Marionberry Pie : Recipes : Cooking Channel." Marionberry Pie :
Recipes : Cooking Channel. Web. 15 Mar. 2015.
<http://www.cookingchanneltv.com/recipes/marionberry-pie.html>.

"Memphis Dry Rub Ribs : Recipes : Cooking Channel." Memphis Dry
Rub Ribs : Recipes : Cooking Channel. Web. 15 Mar. 2015.
<http://www.cookingchanneltv.com/recipes/memphis-dry-rub-ribs.html>.

Mexico, Gayle. "Bacon and Green Chili Quiche Recipe |
Epicurious.com." Web. 14 Mar. 2015.
<http://www.epicurious.com/recipes/food/views/bacon-and-green-chili-quiche-2224>.

"Minnesota State Recipes." Minnesota-Visitor.com. Web. 7 Mar.
2015. <http://www.minnesota-visitor.com/minnesota-state-recipes.html>.

"Minnesota Wild Rice Recipes." Minnesota-Visitor.com. Web. 7 Mar.
2015. <http://www.minnesota-visitor.com/minnesota-wild-rice.html>.

"Mississippi Mud Potatoes Archives - Mama Plus One." Mama Plus
One. Web. 31 May 2015.

"Nebraska Handheld Meat Pies : Recipes : Cooking Channel."
Nebraska Handheld Meat Pies : Recipes : Cooking Channel.
Web. 23 Mar. 2015.
<http://www.cookingchanneltv.com/recipes/nebraska-
handheld-meat-pies.html>.

"Old Time Kentucky Bacon Milk Gravy for Biscuits." Allrecipes.com.
Web. 1 Mar. 2015. <http://allrecipes.com/recipe/old-time-
kentucky-bacon-milk-gravy-for-biscuits/>.

"Our Favorite 2-Ingredient App." RSS. Web. 14 Mar. 2015.
<http://www.popsugar.com/food/Recipe-Bacon-Wrapped-
Dates-4952556>.

"Pancetta Bacon Pasta : Diners, Drive-Ins and Dives : Food Network."
Pancetta Bacon Pasta Recipe : Food Network. Web. 31 May
2015.

"Peanut Butter and Bacon Banana Hot Dogs." Bacon Today. 9 Feb.
2015. Web. 1 Mar. 2015. <http://bacontoday.com/peanut-
butter-and-bacon-banana-hot-dogs/>.

"Pennsylvania Dutch Hot Bacon Dressing Recipe - Food.com."
Pennsylvania Dutch Hot Bacon Dressing Recipe - Food.com.
Web. 31 May 2015.

"Phantom Gourmet -- Bacon Wrapped Lobster." Recipe. Web. 7 Mar.
2015. <https://www.phantomgourmet.com/recipe/bacon-
wrapped-lobster>.

"Philly Cheese Steak : Recipes : Cooking Channel." Philly Cheese
Steak : Recipes : Cooking Channel. Web. 15 Mar. 2015.
<http://www.cookingchanneltv.com/recipes/philly-cheese-
steak.html>.

"Planked Salmon with Honey-Balsamic Glaze : Recipes : Cooking Channel." Planked Salmon with Honey-Balsamic Glaze : Recipes : Cooking Channel. Web. 15 Mar. 2015. <http://www.cookingchanneltv.com/recipes/michael-chiarello/planked-salmon-with-honey-balsamic-glaze.html>.

"Praline Bacon Recipe." - WMC Action News 5. Web. 31 May 2015.

"Potato, Bacon, and Gruyère Soup Recipe | Epicurious.com." Web. 14 Mar. 2015. <http://www.epicurious.com/recipes/food/views/potato-bacon-and-gruyere-soup-11528>.

"Quick Bacon-Cheddar Biscuits : Sunny Anderson : Food Network." Quick Bacon-Cheddar Biscuits Recipe : Sunny Anderson : Food Network. Web. 31 May 2015.

"Recipes." North Carolina Pork Council -. Web. 15 Mar. 2015. <http://www.ncpork.org/apps.ncpork.org/pages/recipes/detail.jsp?recipeid=16>.

"Recipes." North Carolina Pork Council -. Web. 15 Mar. 2015. <http://www.ncpork.org/apps.ncpork.org/pages/recipes/detail.jsp?recipeid=186>.

"RECIPES: Recipe Details." Georgia Peach Burger. Web. 28 Feb. 2015. <http://www.sutterhome.com/recipes/sutter-home-burgerbase-recipes/georgia-peach-burger-0#.VPJG__nF-Sq>.

"Recipes." Pheasant from Pheasant City Lodge. Web. 31 May 2015.

Reinhart, Peter. "Buttermilk Corn Bread with Bacon Recipe | Epicurious.com." Web. 31 May 2015.

"Rhode Island Clam Chowder Recipe." NYT Cooking. Web. 31 May 2015.

"Rose Creek : Fargo, North Dakota." Rose Creek North Dakota : Recipe Exchange. Web. 15 Mar. 2015. <http://www.rosecreek.net/recipe-exchange/?action=recipe_common&itemId=24>.

"Sandra's Alaska Recipes." : SANDRA'S ALASKA CRAB and BACON WRAPS. Web. 28 Feb. 2015. <http://sandrarecipeblogsite.blogspot.com/2010/01/lump-crab-bacon-salad-wraps-serves-4.html#.VPIAtvnF-So>.

"Shrimp and Grits : Recipes : Cooking Channel." Shrimp and Grits : Recipes : Cooking Channel. Web. 15 Mar. 2015. <http://www.cookingchanneltv.com/recipes/shrimp-and-grits.html>.

"Spicy Jalapeno Bacon & Cheese Oysters Recipes." Spicy Jalapeno Bacon & Cheese Oysters Recipes. Web. 28 Feb. 2015. <http://www.shorelifeflorida.com/articles/111-spicy-jalapeno-bacon-cheese-oysters-recipes>.

"Spinach Bacon Egg Casserole." Allrecipes.com. Web. 31 May 2015.

"Storage & Cooking." Virginia Aquaculture Oyster Growers. Web. 31 May 2015.

Stitt, Frank. "Bacon-Infused Carolina Fish Muddle Recipe | Epicurious.com." Web. 31 May 2015.

"Texas Brisket : Recipes : Cooking Channel." Texas Brisket : Recipes : Cooking Channel. Web. 15 Mar. 2015.

<http://www.cookingchanneltv.com/recipes/texas-brisket.html>.

"Texas Style Bacon, Beans and Eggs: Black Bean Chilaquiles : Rachael Ray : Food Network." Texas Style Bacon, Beans and Eggs: Black Bean Chilaquiles Recipe : Rachael Ray : Food Network. Web. 31 May 2015.

"Venison Garlic Bacon Hamburger." Wild Game Recipes NevadaFoodies Elk Recipes Antelope Recipes Duck Recipes and More. Web. 14 Mar. 2015. <http://www.nevadafoodies.com/venison-garlic-bacon-hamburger/>.

"Vermont Baked Beans." Taste of Home. Web. 31 May 2015.

"Virginia Ham Biscuits : Recipes : Cooking Channel." Virginia Ham Biscuits : Recipes : Cooking Channel. Web. 15 Mar. 2015. <http://www.cookingchanneltv.com/recipes/virginia-ham-biscuits.html>.

"WE ARE [INDIANA] BACON." Bacon-Wrapped Shrimp with BBQ Sauce. Web. 1 Mar. 2015. <http://indianakitchenbacon.com/recipes/124>.

Web. 1 Mar. 2015. <http://www.cooks.com/recipe/x77td84f/iowa-corn-chowder.html>.

Web. 14 Mar. 2015. <http://www.nhdairypromo.org/wp-content/uploads/2013/08/Grand-Champion_Tilton-Northfield-Fire-Department.pdf>.

Web. 14 Mar. 2015. <http://www.state.nj.us/dep/fgw/pdf/bear_recipeguide.pdf>.

Web. 15 Mar. 2015. <http://www.cooks.com/recipe/li15q0be/north-dakota-baked-beans.html>.

Web. 7 Mar. 2015. <http://www.cooks.com/recipe/bb57y40u/hot-bacon-salad-dressing.html>.

"West Virginia Pepperoni Roll : Recipes : Cooking Channel." West Virginia Pepperoni Roll : Recipes : Cooking Channel. Web. 15 Mar. 2015. <http://www.cookingchanneltv.com/recipes/west-virginia-pepperoni-roll.html>.

"Wyoming Lamb Stew." Taste of Home. Web. 31 May 2015.

CPSIA information can be obtained
at www.ICGtesting.com
Printed in the USA
FSOW04n1431040316
17701FS

9 781511 406239